THE STOLEN GOLDIN VIOLIN

Mystery at the American Suzuki Institute

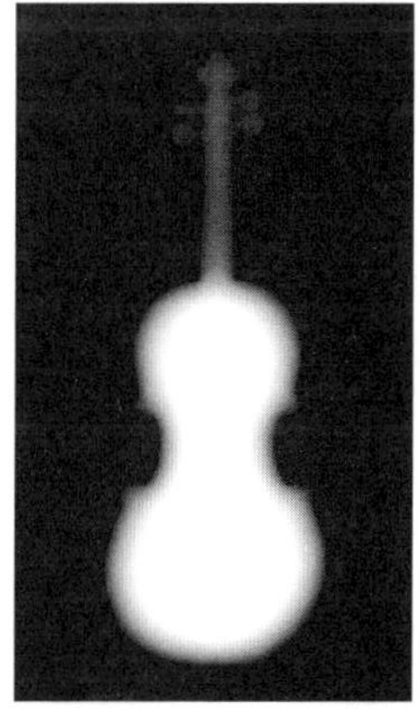

THE STOLEN GOLDIN VIOLIN

Mystery at the American Suzuki Institute

Elizabeth Caulfield Felt
Andy Felt
Craig Felt
Tom Felt

First edition: March 2010

Library of Congress Cataloging-in-Publication Data
Felt, Elizabeth Caulfield
The Stolen Goldin Violin / Elizabeth Caulfield Felt & Andy Felt & Craig Felt & Tom Felt
p. cm.
Summary: During a summer music camp, a mythical "Goldin" violin disappears. Four friends, ages 12 and 13, try to solve the mystery before their week at the American Suzuki Institute is over.
ISBN 978-0-9844507-0-1
[1. Violins—Juvenile Fiction. 2. American Suzuki Institute—Juvenile Fiction. 3. Music Camps—Juvenile Fiction. 4. Violins—Fiction. 5. American Suzuki Institute—Fiction. 6. Music Camps—Fiction. 7. Mystery and Detective Stories.] I. Title.
PZ7.F3367 St 2010
[Fic]-dc22

1 2 3 4 5 6 7 8 9 10

Printed in the United States of America

Published by Elizabeth Caulfield Felt and Andy Felt,

Stevens Point, WI felt.family@yahoo.com

To Gooseberry,
who cannot read, but loves
the sound of the violin.

UW-Stevens Point Map

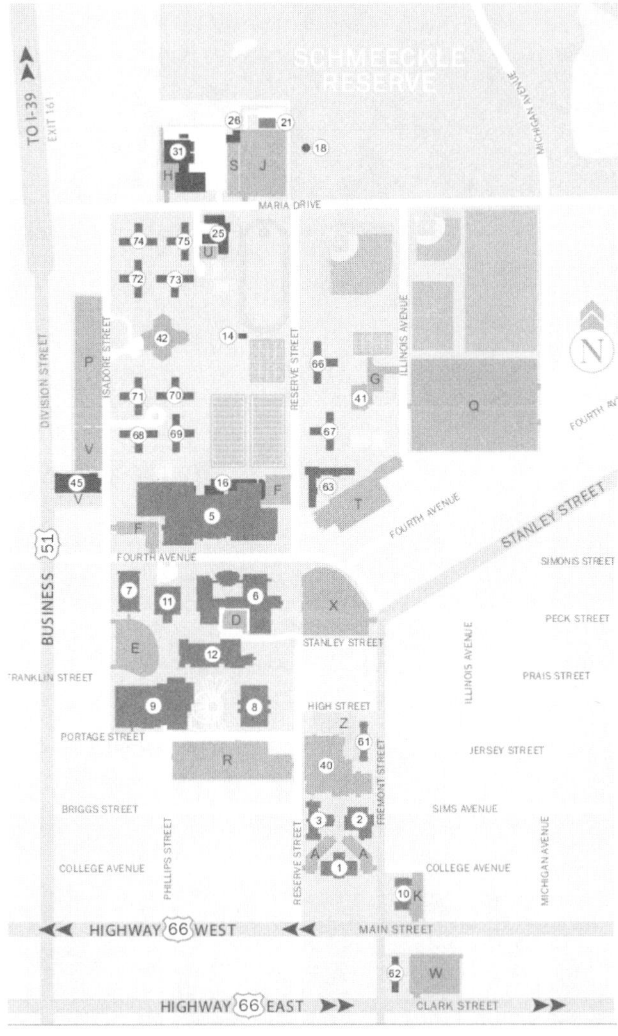

5	Health Enhancement Center (Quandt Gym)		
7	Collins Classroom Center (CCC)	68	Baldwin Hall
9	Noel Fine Arts Center (NFAC)	69	Neale Hall
42	DeBot Center	70	Hansen Hall

Sunday

"Are we almost there?" asked Bayly, looking up from her book.

"It isn't far now," answered her mother. "See, there's the Elizabeth Inn. It's only a few more exits."

"Good," said Bayly. "I've got to pee, but I can make it."

Bayly closed her book and slid it into the backpack at her feet. This would be her fifth year at the American Suzuki Institute in Stevens Point, Wisconsin. Every year she was excited to go, but this year she was more excited than normal.

"I can't believe that by this time tomorrow, I'll have my Goldin violin," said Bayly, twisting her long curly hair around her hand and making a ball of it on top of her head.

"Well, I hope it works out that way," responded Mrs. Hall cautiously.

Bayly let her strawberry blond hair drop. "What do you mean you hope it works out? What wouldn't work out?"

Bayly had wanted a Goldin violin from the time she had seen Joshua Bell play one at Carnegie Hall when she was six years old. She had started taking violin lessons the very next week—late by Suzuki standards. Most Suzuki students started when they were three or four. But, Bayly loved the violin. She practiced two or three hours every day and had caught up with most of her peers who had started at younger ages.

Her polished piece for institute was Corelli's *La Folia*, the first piece in Book 6. Bayly's parents had promised her that if she was still dedicated to the violin when she was large enough for a full-sized violin that they would buy her a Goldin. Bayly was now thirteen and her violin teacher, Mrs. Bishop, had said in the spring that she thought Bayly could move up to a full violin this summer.

"I just want to make sure the violin is right for you before we commit to it, sweetheart," answered Mrs. Hall. "Mrs. Bishop said she would look it over for us Monday afternoon. You know I can't tell the difference between a good violin and great violin. And, at the price the violin maker is asking, this had better be a great violin."

Bayly rolled her eyes. It was a Goldin. Of course it would be a great violin. Augustina Goldin was the premier violin maker in North America. She only made two or three violins a year because she made each by hand, personally, with a special kind of wood that she kept a secret. The wood gave the violin an incredible tone and a very yellow color. Goldin violins were golden, and the very best.

♫

May sat on her bed with all the papers from her registration packet spread out around her. As she read through the material, May absent-mindedly pulled on lengths of her hair, getting used to her new haircut. Her long black hair had been cut two days ago and now fell to a straight line just below her ears. "There is something called the Play-In going on after dinner," May told her mom, who was trying to figure out a way to hang up her clothes without any hangers.

"What time's that?" asked Mrs. Wong.

"Seven. There's kind of a lot of time between dinner and the Play-In. What'll we do?" May's voice wavered a little. Mrs. Wong laid her dresses flat on the dresser and sat down on the single bed across from May's single bed. Their dorm room was small but cozy.

"Don't worry, May. We'll find something fun to do. Maybe you'll make some friends at dinner. Or, if we haven't met anyone, we can walk around campus and figure out which rooms your classes are in." The American Suzuki Institute was held at the University of Wisconsin-Stevens Point, UWSP. The campus seemed small but pretty. Purple and yellow flowers bloomed in patches all around and a variety of trees offered shade. Mrs. Wong and May had retrieved their registration packet in the music building, on the south edge of campus and then walked to their dormitory, Hansen Hall, on the north edge of campus. The walk had taken less than ten minutes.

May nodded and fingered her name badge which included a sparkling silver star to indicate that it was her first year at institute. She had really wanted to come to this violin camp thing, but now that she was here she wasn't sure she should be. She was certain all the other kids would be violin geniuses while she was just average.

Suddenly the door to their room opened and a boy with wild brown hair walked in backward. "I want a room to myself," he was shouting to someone in the hall. "You can share with Dad, but this one's mine."

He turned and his eyes grew enormous when he saw May and Mrs. Wong sitting on their beds. May noticed that his eyes were brown, like his hair, but flecked with gold. He was probably about her age or maybe a little older. The boy did a double take. He looked at the number on the door, then at a paper in his hand and then at the door again.

"I'm sorry," he said, "but I think you're in the wrong room. This room belongs to me, my dad and my little brother." He stepped forward and gave a card to Mrs. Wong.

"Hmmm," murmured Mrs. Wong, looking at the card. She walked over to the desk where she had dropped her own card. "It looks like they have given this room to both of us. We should go get this problem fixed."

At that moment, May noticed a large man standing in the doorway. He had short, salt and pepper hair and dark eyes that looked friendly. "Hunter, what are you doing in these ladies' room?"

Before Hunter could answer, Mrs. Wong stepped forward with the two cards. "Hello, I'm Gloria Wong and this is my daughter May. It looks as though there's been a mistake regarding our rooms."

"Nice to meet you," said the man, offering his hand and smiling. Mrs. Wong shook it. "I'm John Petersen. This rude young fellow is Hunter, and I have another son Blake, somewhere about."

Hunter had sat down on May's bed and was looking through her registration papers. May stood up and moved a little away.

"Hunter, what are you doing?" asked his father.

Instead of answering him, Hunter picked up May's class list and spoke to May, "Hey, we're in the same A class. We've got Gabe Bolkosky. He's awesome; one of the coolest teachers here. Is this your first year at institute? I don't remember seeing you before."

May nodded and quietly asked, "Have you been here before?"

"Oh yeah," said Hunter, picking up a paper and then putting it down and picking up another. "My brother and I come with my dad every year. They've got a pool with this really cool high dive, and on Wednesday night there's a talent show that's always really funny. Have you ever listened to any Nickel Creek? I was listening to them on the drive up. Really, you should hear the violin in this one song."

May was surprised when Hunter grabbed her wrist and gently pulled her out of the room to where his family's bags were stacked in the hall. She saw two violin cases, as well as an assortment of suitcases and backpacks. "My iPod should be in here somewhere," said Hunter, digging through a dark blue Jansport backpack and dumping a deck of cards, a Gameboy and several books and magazines onto the floor.

"May," said Mrs. Wong who was standing in the

hall next to Mr. Petersen, "we're going to go and figure out the room problem. Will you be all right here?"

May could tell her mother was a little nervous to leave her, and normally she would have been nervous too. But, somehow, she didn't feel nervous around Hunter. "I'll be OK. I'm going to stay here and listen to Nickel River."

Hunter laughed so hard he spit all over his backpack. "It's Nickel Creek, not Nickel River."

He was still chuckling when he handed her the ear buds to his iPod.

♫

"Sebastian! Can you come here a minute?"

Sebastian could hear his mom through the Green Day playing on his generic MP3 player. He could pretend not to hear her, but she would probably just get mad. He pulled out his ear buds and walked down the hall.

"What?"

Mrs. Phelps pressed the tape tabs on Greg's diapers, stood him up and gently spanked him. Greg darted out of the room, knocking against Sebastian as he did. The older boy ignored his toddler sibling.

As his mom wrapped up the dirty diaper and stood, she said, "Could you run down to the university and pick up everyone's registration packets? We're supposed to get them by five."

"Can somebody come with me?" Sebastian asked.

Mrs. Phelps walked out of the room to wash her hands. Sebastian followed her down the hall. Over the sound of running water she spoke loudly. "I've got to start getting dinner ready. Dad's mowing the lawn. Maybe you could talk T.J. into going with you."

Sebastian frowned. He hated going places alone, but would going alone be better than going with T.J.? At twelve, Sebastian was the oldest of five kids. T.J. was in the middle at eight. Mostly he was OK, but sometimes he did crazy things to embarrass Sebastian, who was pretty shy. He'd rather take Rachel, who was ten, or Lucy, who was five, but they were both at friends' houses.

"Go where?" T.J. came out of the playroom into the hall, interrupting Sebastian's thoughts.

"Mom wants me to go down and get the registration packets for institute. Wanna come?"

"Can I ride my scooter?" T.J. asked.

"Yeah, I'll ride mine too," said Sebastian.

Bayly and her mother stood in line at the registration desk in the Noel Fine Arts Center, or as everyone called it, the NFAC. This building was home to the UWSP Suzuki program, as well as the university's music, theater and fine arts programs. Behind the registration desk was a large courtyard where colorful and bizarre student sculptures were displayed. They were a variety of shapes, mostly unidentifiable and made from wire, tissue paper, and other materials Bayly couldn't name. The people in front of them at the registration desk took their envelope and Bayly moved forward. "Hall" she said clearly to the woman behind the desk. The woman flipped through some envelopes and as she looked up said, "Jeffrey or—I'm guessing you are Bayly."

Bayly smiled. "Yes. Bayly." The woman smiled and handed Bayly her envelope, then turned her attention to the people standing in the line behind them.

Bayly moved over to an empty table at the edge of the courtyard. "Let's quick look and see what I've got," said Bayly. She held the large brown envelope upside down and emptied its contents onto a small table. There was the program, a newsletter, some smaller pieces of paper. Bayly ignored everything except her class list.

"An eight o'clock!" she groaned. "I've got another eight o'clock class. This is so unfair."

Mrs. Hall laughed. "Everyone has an eight o'clock class, Bayly."

"No, they don't," Bayly argued. "Remember Jasmine from last year? Her first class wasn't until nine."

Mrs. Hall shrugged to indicated she wasn't sure she believed Bayly but wasn't going to argue with her.

Looking back at her class list, Bayly's jaw dropped.

"What is it?" asked her mom.

"Mr. Bolkosky is my A teacher! I can't believe it." Bayly was practically jumping up and down. "Do you remember him? He's cute and got recordings and—"

Just then a little blond boy grabbed her arm. "My brother has Mr. Bolkosky too." He pointed at a boy who must be his brother, a boy the same age as Bayly but with short blond hair, glasses and very red cheeks.

Bayly moved toward him. "I know you. You were in one of my group classes last year, weren't you? Is your name Christian?"

"Sebastian," answered the boy and his brother at the same time.

"Shut up, T.J.," finished the older boy.

"So, you have Mr. Bolkosky for A class too?"

Sebastian nodded. "I had him for B class a couple of years ago. He's really cool."

"I just wish it weren't at eight," said Bayly.

Sebastian nodded. There was an awkward silence while everyone stood by each other but nobody said anything.

"Well, see you tomorrow, bright and early," said Bayly.

"See you," said Sebastian, grabbing his brother's arm and pulling him toward a door on the other side of the courtyard.

As they left, Bayly could hear Sebastian's brother say, "She's pretty. I think you should kiss her."

Bayly looked at her mom and they both laughed.

♫

May's mom and Hunter's dad fixed the room problem. The Wongs got to keep their room and the Petersen family had rooms across and next door to them. Walking back to their dormitory, Mrs. Wong asked Mr. Petersen if there were any good places to run, and they discovered that they were both morning joggers. Mr. Petersen described the Schmeeckle Reserve, just a block or so from their dormitory, which included a nature trail around beautiful Lake Joanis.

When they returned to Hansen Hall, Mr. Petersen went into his new room and came back with a handful of hangars for Mrs. Wong.

"My room has more than we need," he said.

The families ate dinner together in the DeBot cafeteria and then gathered their instruments for the short walk to the Play-In. May couldn't believe how easy it had been to make a friend. Hunter pretty much talked all the time, so it didn't matter that she was usually shy. Plus, he was able to teach her all sorts of things about institute since he'd been here before.

"So, what exactly is A class?" asked May.

"Oh, that's the small class," said Hunter, bending down and picking up a long blade of grass from beside the sidewalk. "There are only three or four people in A class. Then B class is a little bigger with the same A class people plus some others, then C class is even bigger with all the people from B class plus others, and then D class is orchestra."

"So, we'll have all the same classes?" asked May surprised.

"Of course." Hunter used the blade of grass to tickle the back of his little brother's neck, who was walking a little in front of them with a group of boys his own age. Blake kept moving his hand to swat his neck as though chasing a fly away. Finally, Blake realized what was happening. He turned around and gave Hunter a look that said, "You are so immature," then moved around his friends so that he wasn't near his brother any more.

At ten, Blake was three years younger than Hunter, but in some ways he seemed older. His brown hair was short and neat, and he acted pretty serious. Hunter, on the other hand, had wild hair, a relaxed attitude and seemed a little messy about everything. May was curious to hear him play the violin.

"It's that building right there," said Hunter.

The Play-In was in the Quandt Gym where the UWSP basketball team played. A stage had been set up on one side of the gym. Some bleacher seats were pulled out and folding chairs were arranged all across the middle of the gym facing the stage. There was also a balcony with more bleachers.

"You wanna sit up there?" asked Hunter pointing at the balcony.

May didn't want to go so far away. "Let's sit behind our parents," she said.

Hunter shrugged and they sat down, putting their violin cases on the floor in front of them. Blake sat in the front row with his friends.

Before the Play-In started, there was a welcome ceremony. Pat D'Ercole, the director of the institute, introduced people and announced the winners of some scholarships. After those people had walked on stage, the director started naming all the places institute teachers and students were from.

"I believe this year the farthest anyone traveled to come here is from Australia."

Hunter and May looked at each other with wide eyes.

"There are more than twenty students and teachers from outside the United States this year. Clap your hands if you traveled from outside North America."

May looked around to see who was clapping. She saw a family who looked like they were from India: the woman wore a sari and the daughter had beautiful long black hair.

"We have people from Mexico," continued the director. It sounded like only one or two people clapped. "From Canada," lots of clapping. "And, our Americans come from lots of places too. We have a number of people from California and Washington." May started clapping.

Hunter looked at her. "Are you from California or Washington?"

"California," May answered. She held up her name badge which said "San Diego, CA" under her name.

"Wow," said Hunter. "Did you fly in a plane to get here?"

May nodded.

"We're just from—" but before he could say, the director was saying Minnesota and Hunter was standing up, clapping and whooping.

"Minneapolis," Hunter finished.

After the announcements, the director told people who played instruments other than the violin where they should go for their Play-Ins. The violins stayed in the gym.

"What exactly is the Play-In?" May asked Hunter as they both opened their cases and got their violins out.

Hunter shrugged. "We just stand around and play. The director will name a piece and say which teacher will lead it. If you know it you play it, and if you don't you don't."

They got tuned up and stood in an open space behind the folding chairs. The first piece announced was *Humoresque.* As May played she looked all around the room. She couldn't believe how many violinists were there, all playing the same piece. Some kids were really little too. Over to her right was a little girl who didn't look any older than four or five and she was playing *Humoresque*!

The next piece was *Go Tell Aunt Rhody*, then the first movement of the Vivaldi Concerto in A minor. When they announced Fiocco's *Allegro* Hunter and May both put their violins under their arms.

Hunter grabbed May's shoulder and turned her around. "Look! Do you see her up in the balcony?"

May squinted toward the balcony. "Who?"

"There, right there. It's Selena Montoya."

May laughed. "Selena Montoya isn't going to be here."

"Don't you see her?" said Hunter. His voice was serious and urgent.

May could tell who he meant. There was a teenage girl who looked a lot like Selena Montoya, the star of one of the Disney Channel's most popular new television shows. She was playing the violin up on the balcony, standing next to a very tall, very skinny boy with spiky orange hair.

"Well, she looks a little like Selena Montoya," said May, "but there is no way she is Selena Montoya."

Hunter was nodding his head confidently. "It's Selena Montoya. I read on the internet that she is a really good musician and plays several instruments.

I've got a poster of her in my room at home. That is definitely Selena Montoya."

May laughed.

The piece ended and May and Hunter stared at the teenage Selena and the boy next to her.

"Do you really think Selena Montoya would have a boyfriend like that?" asked May.

"What makes you think that's her boyfriend?"

May shrugged. "She's standing really close to him."

The next piece was the first movement of Bach's Concerto for Two Violins in D minor — the Bach Double. May loved the Bach Double, and it was so fun to play with a room full of violinists, half playing the first part and half playing the second.

The Play-In finished with the *Twinkle* parade. All the violinists joined a moving line and walked around the gym, in and out of the gym, up to the balcony and back down, all the while playing the *Twinkle* variations.

When the parade was over, May and Hunter met back at their violin cases. Hunter sighed in a dreamy way. "I can't believe I'm in the same building as Selena Montoya. That boy isn't her boyfriend, because I'm going to be her boyfriend."

May chortled. Mrs. Wong appeared and picked up May's violin case just as May finished zipping it shut. "We need to get back to our room and get some sleep. We have to get up early tomorrow."

"Yes, Mama." May turned to Hunter, who was staring up at the balcony and who hadn't put his violin or bow away yet. "See you tomorrow, Hunter."

"Good night, May."

Monday

Sebastian walked slowly behind the disorderly mob that was his family. They lived just a few blocks from campus, so they always walked to institute. In one hand Sebastian carried his violin and in his other he held Greg's hand. Greg was the only Phelps child not attending institute, but he had to come because at two and a half, he was too young to stay home alone. His dad was pulling the wagon that contained T.J.'s cello and a cooler with their lunches and a bag with swimsuits and towels. Lucy was holding Mom's hand and Rachel and T.J. were arguing about something. T.J. pushed Rachel, who fell into the wagon and almost knocked the cello out. Dad grabbed T.J. and pulled him up in front of everyone. Rachel fell into step beside Sebastian.

"What's your first class?" asked Rachel.

"A. What's yours?"

"B, but not 'til nine. I hope I know somebody."

Sebastian nodded, then remembered that he did know somebody in his A class, sort of. She had asked his name, but he didn't know her name. Man, he hoped she hadn't heard what T.J. said.

When they got to the NFAC they split up. Mom was going to go with Lucy to her viola class, Dad was going with T.J. to his cello class, and Rachel was supposed to entertain Greg in the hall outside Lucy's class. Sebastian's first class was in a different building. He said good-bye to everyone, although nobody seemed to notice, and then slipped out the door toward the CCC.

When Sebastian walked into his A classroom, all the other students were already there.

The girl from yesterday was talking with the other kids, and the parents were sitting in chairs looking sleepy. The girl's long curly hair was still wet from her shower, and Sebastian noticed for the first time how tall she was, standing with the other students. He looked at her name tag and saw her name was Bayly. The tiny Asian girl was May and a boy with messy brown hair was Hunter. Sebastian put his case on a desk-chair and started getting his violin out.

He overheard Bayly talking in a sort of arrogant voice, "Mr. Harry was in California last weekend, so he brought it with him and I'm going to pick it up today."

The other girl said, "Wow, a Goldin."

Sebastian put his violin under his arm and walked over to where the kids were talking.

Hunter said, "So, what's so special about a Goldin? Is it made of gold?"

The two girls stared at him, then Bayly turned to Sebastian, "You know what a Goldin violin is, don't you?"

Sebastian could feel his cheeks turning red. He hated being put on the spot like this. He'd heard of golden violins before, but he wasn't sure what they were exactly.

"I guess," he tried as an answer.

Bayly barely heard him and faced Hunter. "Goldin violins are the best violins being made today. Augustina Goldin makes each by hand with this special wood that she won't tell anyone about. They have fabulous tone and are incredibly beautiful. I can't wait to try mine out."

"Bayly, come here," said one of the moms, sitting in a chair against the wall balancing a coffee cup on her knee. Bayly's mom kind of whispered, but everyone could hear what she said. "Will you stop already about the Goldin? It's getting to the point where you are almost being rude. Promise me you won't say another word about it until we are certain you are getting it."

Bayly pursed her lips. "But Mom—"

"I mean it. Not another word."

Just then their teacher walked in the door. "Sorry I'm late. I went to the NFAC by mistake. Before we tune up and get started, let's all get to know each other. I'm Gabe Bolkosky, I'm seventeen years old, I live in Ann Arbor, Michigan, my favorite composer is Kreisler, I teach violin and have a dwarf hidden in my luggage."

The girls both giggled.

"So, let's start with you," said Gabe pointing at Sebastian. "Tell us your name, where you live, your age, your favorite composer or piece, and anything else you might think is important."

Sebastian cleared his throat and then spoke, "My name is Sebastian Phelps. I live here in Stevens Point, I'm twelve years old, my favorite composer is Vivaldi, and um, I have two sisters and one brother at the institute so neither of my parents will be able to come to this class."

"Well, that's too bad. You'll have to introduce them to me at some other time. Nice to meet you, Sebastian. Next," said Mr. Bolkosky.

The boy standing next to Sebastian spoke, "I'm Hunter Petersen, I'm thirteen years old, I don't really have a favorite composer, and that's my dad and little brother over there."

"Nice to meet you, Hunter."

"I'm Bayly Hall," said Bayly. "I live in Chicago, I just turned thirteen in June, my favorite piece is Corelli's *Courant*, and ... and," Bayly frowned and looked at her mother. "I just moved up to a full-sized violin. The one I have today is my backup violin to keep at school for orchestra and stuff but it's a pretty cheap violin. I'm getting a better one very soon."

Mr. Bolkosky nodded. "It's easier to sound good when playing a good violin, but there are a lot of little things one can do to make a cheap violin play to its potential." Mr. Bolkosky looked at Bayly and raised his left eyebrow. "Do you play the *Courant*?"

Bayly laughed. "Not yet."

"Nice to meet you, Bayly."

"I'm May Wong," said May so quietly Sebastian almost couldn't hear. "I'm from San Diego, I'm twelve years old and my favorite piece is the Bach Double."

"Which part do you like to play?" asked Mr. Bolkosky.

"The first," answered May.

"Of course!" said Mr. Bolkosky raising his arms in the air and holding his violin and bow up high. "So, who wants to go first?"

At first nobody did anything, but then Bayly stepped forward.

Bayly's polished piece was *La Folia*. Sebastian groaned inside. His piece was *La Folia* too. Bayly played it all the way through. She played well, but her tone was flat, probably from the cheap violin more than because she had done anything wrong. As she played, Mr. Bolkosky took notes. When she was done, everyone applauded.

Mr. Bolkosky put his fingertips together, placing his thumbs on his chin and his pointer fingers on his nose. "Lovely, lovely," he said. "You know, Bayly, as you were playing, I was seeing your performance as a painting. The detail was marvelous. Each of your notes was like a brush stroke, accurate and precise, you didn't miss a note and your fingers landed in precisely the right spots. Your dynamics were the people in the painting, and they seemed to move and breathe. You gave life to your music, which you passed on to your audience. Your colors are bright, but not as vibrant as they could be, and there's a bit of shadow in the corner. Why do you think that is, Bayly?"

Bayly wrinkled her brow. "My tone?" she asked.

Mr. Bolkosky nodded. "Perhaps."

"My three-quarters violin had a much better tone, but this violin isn't very good. I'd have played it better on a better violin."

Mr. Bolkosky continued nodding but said, "You can't blame the violin entirely. I think you didn't expect to get a brilliant tone, and so you didn't push your instrument. Think about full bows, making them strong and long."

He had her play several sections of *La Folia*, focusing on strong, long bows.

Soon Bayly's lesson was finished and then it was May's turn.

Just as May was getting ready to play, a cell phone blasted *The 1812 Overture.* Bayly turned toward her mom. Mrs. Hall blushed and apologized. She reached into her purse and fumbled around. The noise stopped.

"That was amazing," said Mr. Bolkosky. "May, how did you get your violin to do that?" Everyone laughed.

May's polished piece was the first movement of Handel's Sonata in F minor. Sebastian was impressed with May's playing. Her violin wasn't very big, maybe even just a one-half, but she got a really big sound out of it. Mr. Bolkosky praised parts of May's playing, and prodding May to find her weak spots, offered her exercises that would help strengthen her piece.

Hunter was after May. "When did you start playing the violin, Mr. Bolkosky?" he asked as he stepped forward and May sat down.

"I started when I was four, with a Suzuki teacher. What piece are you planning to play for us, Hunter?"

"*Gigue*," answered Hunter. "Don't you have a bunch of recordings? Did you bring any that we could buy?"

Mr. Bolkosky smiled patiently. "I have made some recordings and I do have some I could sell to you, but I think, right now it is time for the focus to be on you and *Gigue*."

With a little more prodding, Mr. Bolkosky finally got Hunter to start. Once Hunter started, he played well. Sebastian noticed how focused his eyes seemed as he played.

Sebastian went last. He'd been playing *La Folia* every day for the past few weeks to make sure it was ready for institute, and he thought he played it pretty well. Mr. Bolkosky praised his energy and his focus and his tone.

"What do you need to improve in this piece?" Mr. Bolkosky asked Sebastian.

Sebastian paused, although he knew the answer. "The runs," he finally said.

Mr. Bolkosky nodded. "You want to practice them slowly. I know, it can be hard to play them extremely slowly, but try. Play them as slowly as you possibly can. Until it is so slow it is painful. Then, when you can play each note, clear and strong, go a tiny bit faster, little by little. Tomorrow, I want to see how slowly you can play those last runs, starting on measure," he checked his book, "measure 184."

"OK," said Sebastian.

He took a bow and the class was over. Mr. Bolkosky rushed out the door, apologizing and saying that he had another class in just a few minutes in the NFAC.

"Are you going to get your Goldin now?" May asked Bayly as she snapped shut her case.

"If Harry's is open," she answered. "Want to come?"

"Can I?" May asked her mom.

"Sure."

They climbed the stairs to the large second floor classroom that acted as Harry's music store for the duration of institute. The store was empty except for two adults who had their backs to them, moving cases and boxes around and getting things organized.

"Janet, this is the last of the stuff. I'll run down and move the van before I get a ticket," said the man. "Can you handle the store?"

"No problem."

The man greeted May and Bayly and their moms as he left the room, saying, "Janet can help you with anything you need."

The store had obviously just opened. Long tables were set in the shape of an L. Instruments, books and musical paraphernalia were being displayed on the tables, but Bayly's eyes went straight to the bottom of the L, where an open case held what had to be a Goldin violin.

"There it is!" gasped Bayly.

She walked over to the case and pulled the violin out.

"Wait a minute," said Janet hurrying over. "That's not really for sale. It's a special order for someone."

Bayly smiled. "It's a special order for me. I'm Bayly Hall."

"Oh," said Janet looking a little surprised. "Wow. Is it going to be your first full size?"

"Yeah," said Bayly. She was looking at the violin lovingly, caressing its sides. The yellow wood glowed as though it were lit from within. May could tell Bayly wanted to play it, but there was no chin rest and the case did not have a bow.

Bayly's mom stepped forward. "Mrs. Bishop, Bayly's home teacher, is going to meet us here at noon, so she can look it over with us, but Bayly wanted to see it as soon as you opened."

Janet smiled. "I don't blame her. It's a gorgeous violin. Here, let me get a chin rest for you, and we'll try to find a bow you can use."

Janet walked around, opening cases and looking inside boxes. Finally, she came back, handed Bayly a chin rest and began rosining a bow. While Bayly was putting on the chin rest, Janet said, "The violin comes with that case, but not with a chin rest or bow, so you may want to think about buying those here too. We don't have a wide bow selection in this store, but we do have two or three really good ones. With such an excellent violin, you wouldn't want to skimp on the bow."

Mrs. Hall turned to Mrs. Wong, "I hadn't given a single thought to the bow."

Mrs. Wong nodded, "A good bow can make a big difference in sound quality."

Bayly had already gotten the chin rest fastened and was tuning the violin. When she was satisfied, she started playing the second movement of Vivaldi's Concerto in G minor.

The tone of the Goldin was deep and pure, like a strong warm wind. It took May's breath away.

Bayly switched to *Country Dance*, and goosebumps ran up May's arm.

Mrs. Hall said, "I'm not really very musical, but I can tell that is an amazing violin."

Mrs. Wong answered, "Second only to the Stradivarius. My husband and I met Augustina Goldin at a fund raising dinner for the San Diego Symphony a few years ago. She's a rather strange woman, but she certainly makes a fine violin."

"Strange how?" asked Mrs. Hall.

Mrs. Wong laughed. "She reminded me of a female Albert Einstein: wild white hair, skinny, and a sort of vacant look in her eye. Well, not vacant, but like she was not aware of what was going on around her—like she was thinking about much greater things and couldn't be bothered with the average person. Eccentric is maybe the right word."

Bayly had stopped playing. "Can't we just buy it now, Mom, so I can play it at my next lesson?"

Mrs. Hall laughed. "You can wait another three hours, Bayly. Besides, I need to talk to Mrs. Bishop about what sort of bow we need to get to go with it. Do you like the one you're using right now?"

Bayly shrugged, "I guess so."

Mrs. Hall looked up at the clock in the room. It was almost 9:30. "I wonder if there's somewhere close by where I could get a cup of coffee before the next lesson."

Mrs. Wong said, "The cafeteria isn't too far."

Mrs. Hall shook her head. "We didn't sign up for the meal plan."

Janet offered, "There's a gas station on the corner of Division and Fourth. It's just a block away and their coffee isn't too bad."

Mrs. Hall frowned at the idea of gas station coffee, but then said, "I guess I'll run down there and try it. Bayly, do you want to come with me or do you want to stay with May and I'll just meet you at your next class?"

"I'll go with May," said Bayly, reluctantly putting the Goldin back in its case. "Hey, Mom, when your cell phone went off right when May was getting ready to play, who was it? Was it Dad?"

Mrs. Hall touched May gently on the shoulder, "Oh! I'm so sorry about that. I can't believe I forgot to turn it off. You know, I didn't check to see who it was." She pulled the phone out of her purse and checked her messages. Snapping it shut, she said, "Just a wrong number. United Airlines said I left a bag on board my plane."

Bayly laughed. "We didn't take a plane."

"Nope. I better run if I'm going to make it to your next class on time. See you there."

Mrs. Hall dashed out the door, and the others started slowly walking to the NFAC and their C class, Bayly talking nonstop about the beauty of the Goldin violin.

The C class consisted of about twenty-five or thirty violinists, some slightly more advanced than Bayly and her friends and some slightly less advanced. The teacher talked about school and practice and after school activities and the importance of priorities. They played a number of pieces, focusing on the dynamics in specific places.

After class, Hunter put his violin away very quickly. “The pool’s open now, are you coming swimming?” he asked the others.

May shrugged. “Yeah, I guess so.”

Sebastian nodded. “My whole family is planning to go.”

Bayly shook her head. “Mrs. Bishop is going to meet us at Harry’s to look over my Goldin. Maybe I can show it to you all at orchestra.”

“Great!” said May. “See you there.”

♫

Hunter grabbed his goggles and headed for the door. “Wait, Hunter,” said Mr. Petersen. “You need to put your clothes and shoes in the locker so I can lock them up.”

Hunter threw his shoes in the bottom of the locker and tossed his clothes in on top of them.

Blake and his father looked at each other, shaking their heads, and hung their own clothes on the hooks in the locker.

“Beat ya out there, Blake,” said Hunter slipping out of the locker room.

“Yes, you will,” answered Blake.

The pool was one of Hunter’s favorite parts of institute. He and Blake had been to a few other violin camps, but none of them were as much fun because they didn’t have a pool.

Blake got in line to do the swim test so that he could swim in the deep end. The pool was really two pools: a shallow pool for lap swimming and playing around—there was a basketball hoop on one side—and a deep pool with two regular diving boards and between them, a very tall diving board, "the high dive." Hunter liked to play basketball and horse around in the pool, but diving was his favorite. At home he was on the YMCA swim team but there wasn't a diving team until high school. He couldn't wait until he could join that team and be allowed to do twists and somersaults.

After passing the swim test, he went straight to the diving board and did a one and a half somersault in pike position. When his head came up out of the water, he heard a whistle. The life guard was telling him that somersaults were not allowed. Hunter groaned. He'd hoped they'd changed the rules this year.

"Hunter!" He turned and saw May, Sebastian, and a girl who was probably Sebastian's sister sitting on the side of the pool. Hunter swam over to them.

"Great dive," said May.

"Thanks. Wanna go off the high dive?" Hunter said, pulling himself out of the water and sitting on the side of the pool next to Sebastian.

May and Sebastian both frowned, but the other girl said, "Sure."

May hesitated. "Have you done it before? It looks awfully high."

"Sure, I do it every year," said Hunter.

"It isn't really that high," said the other girl.

"OK," said May standing up. "Coming?" she asked Sebastian.

Sebastian's sister laughed. "He's afraid of the high dive."

"No, I'm not," said Sebastian. "It's just that without my glasses, it's hard to see and all. I'm not afraid."

"Whatever," said his sister.

The three kids went to the high dive, leaving Sebastian at the side of the pool. He watched as first Hunter, then his sister Rachel, then May jumped off the high board. Rachel screamed as she jumped, though Sebastian knew she wasn't afraid. When each kid hit the water, there was a smacking sound that Sebastian imagined must hurt. The truth was, he was afraid. It was just so high! If a person did a belly flop from that high it would probably kill them.

They got out of the pool close to the ladder and did the high dive again. This time when they climbed out of the pool, Sebastian could tell they were arguing about something. Hunter pointed to the tall diving board and May pointed to the other board. Rachel pointed to the lower one too, and they all went over to the regular diving board.

Sebastian stood up and joined them at the back of the line. In the front, Hunter said, "Let's play copy cat. You have to do whatever I do."

Rachel said, "But you aren't allowed to do somersaults."

Hunter opened his mouth wide. "How did you know I was going to do a somersault?"

May and Rachel both laughed.

Hunter said, "No somersaults."

He climbed the steps and at top speed ran off the diving board. When he was over the water, he shook his body like he was having convulsions and screamed, "Aaahh!" His back smacked the water as he went in.

"Do you think that hurt?" asked May.

"Not much," said Rachel, but I'm not going to lean back so much. Then she climbed on the board and ran off shaking and screaming.

When it was Sebastian's turn, he made such a goofy face as he went into the water that all the kids laughed and made him go first for the next round of copy cat.

♫

Bayly's arms and legs were humming and hard to control as she hurried down the hall toward Harry's. She didn't think she'd ever been this excited about anything. Her mother and Mrs. Bishop were behind her, walking slowly and discussing bows. Bayly didn't care about the bow; she just wanted her Goldin.

The room was much more crowded than it had been that morning. A young boy was playing a violin over on one side of the room, while his parents talked. A group of teens was looking over something in a box, and Mr. Harry was standing behind the table talking to another teen. Bayly didn't see Janet.

Mr. Harry and the teen stopped talking, and Bayly walked over to the store owner. "Is Janet here?" she asked.

"She's having lunch," said Mr. Harry. "Can I help you with something?"

Bayly smiled so big she thought her lips would crack. "I'm here to get my Goldin."

Mr. Harry smiled back. "You must be Bayly. Janet told me you were in earlier. You are one lucky girl. Let's see what we can do for you." Mr. Harry started looking through violin cases and moving things around behind the tables.

Her mom and Mrs. Bishop were in the store now, standing behind Bayly. They were talking about some lecture they were both planning to go to later.

Bayly walked over to where the Goldin had been before, but there was nothing on that part of the table. "It was right here," said Bayly.

An older man with gray hair and a boy Bayly's age tried to get Mr. Harry's attention.

"I'll be with you in a minute," said Mr. Harry.

He paused and looked off in the distance, like he was trying to think hard. "That's funny," he said. "I know I had it right here." He turned around and bent over again, moving cases and boxes and looking all around.

Bayly felt like she was going to throw up. Why couldn't he find it? She searched the cases with her eyes, but they all looked the same. The Goldin had been in a case with a blue velvet interior, but the outside had been rectangular and black like most violin cases.

Mr. Harry stood up straight again. "Let me call Janet. Maybe she put it aside somewhere." He took out a cell phone and started dialing. A woman moved in next to Bayly and, holding up some rosin, said to Mr. Harry, "Can I pay for this?"

Mr. Harry nodded and made his way to the cash register. Bayly followed. As he worked the cash register, he started talking. Bayly could only hear Mr. Harry's half of the conversation, with pauses when Janet was obviously talking.

"Hi Janet. Bayly Hall is here to get her Goldin, but I can't seem to find it. Did you move it somewhere special? ... No, there's nothing on that part of the table." Finished helping the rosin lady and still talking on the phone, Mr. Harry walked back to where the Goldin should be. "No, not there either. ... Are you sure? ... Uh huh. About an hour ago, but it was the one for him. ... I don't know. Well, come back as soon as you can. They're right here. ... OK. ... Well, you can't help that. ... OK. Thanks."

Mr. Harry closed his phone and made a sort of half smile. "Well, Janet doesn't know where it is either. After you played it this morning, she said she just left it out where it was. But, as you can see, it isn't here anymore."

Now Bayly really thought she was going to throw up. She turned to her mom. "Don't worry, Bayly, I'm sure it will turn up." Mrs. Hall turned to Mr. Harry, "When should we come back?"

"Well, I can't look too well right now, with so many customers in the store. I was going to close up at 12:30 and go to lunch. I'll just pick something up and find your Goldin. Can you be back at two o'clock?"

Bayly looked at the schedule on the back of her name tag. She had orchestra at one o'clock and B class at two o'clock. "No, I've got a class."

At the same time Bayly spoke, Mrs. Bishop said,

"I can make two o'clock."

Mrs. Hall said, "I know I shouldn't skip your B class, but this is a special situation. I'll meet Mrs. Bishop here, and we'll get everything straightened out, and you can meet us here after your class."

Bayly nodded but looked unhappy.

"Great!" said Mr. Harry. "I'm really sorry for the mess-up, but by two o'clock we'll have it all figured out."

♫

When Bayly got to orchestra, she saw an empty seat next to May and sat down. Right away, May said, "Did you get the Goldin? Is your mom going to let you play it now?"

Bayly had to take a deep breath so she wouldn't cry.

"Somebody stole my Goldin," she muttered. Sebastian and Hunter, sitting in front of them, turned around.

"Somebody stole your Goldin?!" shouted Hunter.

Bayly nodded and shrugged all at the same time. "It's not there any more. Mr. Harry acted like he was going to find it, but they left it out on the table. Remember where it was, May? It was on a table close to the back door. Anybody could have come in, closed it up and walked off with it while Mr. Harry and Janet were busy helping people."

Sebastian said, "It can get pretty crazy in Harry's sometimes, but who do you think would sneak in and steal it?"

Bayly looked up and snorted. "Only someone who loves playing the violin, knows how good a Goldin is, and can't afford to buy one."

Hunter laughed. "Like just about everybody attending institute."

"You don't know for sure it was stolen, do you?" asked May.

Bayly sniffed. "Harry's going to close up for lunch and look for it. My mom and violin teacher are going to go back at 2:00 and see if he could find it, but I don't think he will. I'm sure someone stole it."

They heard a rapping noise at the front of the room. Mr. Poffinbarger, the orchestra teacher, was tapping his baton on a music stand.

"I'm Mr. Poffinbarger, but you can call me Mr. P." Mr. P. had a sort of goatee beard thing and long hair pulled back into a ponytail. "I'm going to pass out music now, and just accept the part that you get. Everyone here is a talented musician, so we're just going to play parts based on where you're sitting."

Sebastian leaned over toward Hunter. "Mr. P. is my orchestra teacher at school. He's really cool."

Hunter nodded. "I had him for orchestra last year."

Bayly was relieved when she was handed a first violin part. At least something was going right today.

♫

While May was in orchestra, Mrs. Wong chatted with some of the parents and learned about the practice rooms on the third floor of the NFAC. She went up, explored the practice room area, and signed May up for a room at 3:00. So, while Bayly, Hunter and Sebastian all ran to Harry's to find out what had happened with Bayly's Goldin, May was climbing the stairs to her practice room.

Although she was a little angry with her mother, May did want to get her practice over with. She had homework from each of her classes: special things that each teacher had asked them to work on. May started with the Handel sonata.

When her time with the room was up, May followed her mom down the narrow hallway to the stairs. She glanced in a window of one of the practice rooms and was surprised to see Mr. Bolkosky. It looked like he was playing a Goldin. She stopped suddenly and looked again. Somebody else was in the room and had moved, and that person's back was blocking the little window in the door. May stood still, hoping that person would move again so she could see.

Instead, the person turned and started opening the door. May jumped and ran forward to catch up with her mother. "Just a minute, Mama, I need to tie my shoe." May bent down and turned her head so she could see behind her. Mr. Bolkosky and a woman both exited the practice room, each of them carrying a violin case. They walked the other way down the hall.

"May, you're wearing sandals," said Mrs. Wong, puzzled.

"Oh, sorry. Let's go."

They walked down to the second floor where the four o'clock concert in Michelsen Hall would be held.

"I'm going to run to the bathroom quick. Do you need to go?" asked Mrs. Wong.

"No," said May. "I'll wait for you here."

May looked down the wide hall to a big staircase in a sort of funky design. Instead of having walls or half walls along the steps, the staircase was open, and under the handrails and under the guardrails at each landing ran lengths of strong, silver cable. The design, and the windows at the end of the hall, gave the area a vast open feel. As May gazed at the staircase, she saw two people come down the steps: Mr. Bolkosky and the woman who had been in the practice room with him. They chatted at the second floor level, then said goodbye. The woman continued down the stairs and Mr. Bolkosky headed in May's direction.

May's heart started pounding. She had to ask. She just had to.

As he got closer, she said, "Hi, Mr. Bolkosky."

He was looking toward the concert hall and didn't hear her.

May took a deep breath and said as loudly as she could, "Hi, Mr. Bolkosky."

He turned and noticed her. "Hi, May. Are you going to the four o'clock concert?"

"Um, yeah. I'm waiting for my mom." May nodded her head toward the bathrooms. Then she just spit it out,"Mr. Bolkosky, do you own a Goldin violin?"

He gave her a funny look, squinting his eyes and tipping his head a little. "Why would you ask a question like that?"

May could feel her heart beating in her ears. "I just wondered."

"No, May, I do not own a Goldin violin." There was an awkward pause and then he said, "Enjoy the concert." Mr. Bolkosky walked away and into the concert hall.

As her eyes followed Mr. Bolkosky, May saw Bayly, Hunter and Sebastian in the couch area just outside Michelsen Hall.

She ran over to them. "Well?" said May. But then she realized she shouldn't have asked. Bayly's eyes were red and puffy.

"They couldn't find it," said Hunter. "Mr. Harry finally called the police and reported it stolen."

May sat on the couch next to Hunter. Nobody said anything, until May felt like she had to.

"I've got to tell you guys what just happened."

"Yeah?" asked Hunter.

"When I was done practicing upstairs, I walked by a practice room and I saw Mr. Bolkosky playing a Goldin. I mean, I'm pretty sure he was playing a Goldin. And then someone blocked my view and I couldn't see him anymore. Then, just now, I saw him again and I asked him if he owned a Goldin and he acted really funny and said no."

May stopped talking and everyone stared at her.

"You think Mr. Bolkosky stole my Goldin?" said Bayly in disbelief.

"No, I didn't say that," said May. "I was just telling you what I saw."

"Mr. Bolkosky wouldn't steal a Goldin," said Bayly. "If he wanted one, I'm sure he would just buy one."

Sebastian and May looked at each other. "I doubt he could afford a Goldin," said Sebastian while May nodded.

"What?" said Hunter. "He's got like recordings and stuff. I'm sure he could afford a Goldin."

"I don't know," said Sebastian. "He's mostly a teacher and teachers don't make much money. And even though he makes and sells recordings, that doesn't mean he's rich. It isn't like rock and roll music. My mom teaches voice here at the university, and she sells recordings of her singing, but she doesn't make much money at all."

Hunter turned toward Bayly. "What do your parents do?"

"They're both doctors."

Everyone nodded.

"It's hard to imagine him stealing a violin, though," said May.

"Well," said Bayly, "maybe he wasn't planning to, but maybe he went into Harry's and saw it there, and realized nobody was watching, and then couldn't help himself." Bayly almost could see herself stealing a Goldin if she had the opportunity.

"We should keep an eye on him," said Hunter, "and see if we can catch him with the Goldin."

"If he's got it," said May, "it's in the case he carried into the concert hall."

Mrs. Wong walked up. "We better go in and get seats," she said to May.

"I've got to go home," said Sebastian standing up. "I'm supposed to babysit at 4:30."

"Can you come back later tonight?" asked Hunter.

"I don't know," said Sebastian. "Where will you be?"

"Give me your cell number," said Hunter pulling his phone out of his pocket.

"I don't have a cell phone," said Sebastian.

"Then call me," said Hunter and he gave Sebastian the number.

Bayly pulled out her phone and put Hunter's and Sebastian's numbers into it too.

"I don't feel like going to the concert," she said. "I'm going to my room and lie down, but I'll call you later. Keep an eye on Mr. Bolkosky and call me if you find out anything." She gave her number and left.

Hunter followed Mrs. Wong and May into the concert hall. It was dark inside, although the concert hadn't started yet. Most of the seats were taken. He looked around and then heard his name.

"Hunter!" whisper-shouted his dad. He saw that his dad and brother had saved him a seat. "I'll see you back at the dorm," Hunter said to May who was following her mother to two empty seats in the middle of a row near the back.

"OK."

Hunter walked down to the empty seat next to his dad, searching for Mr. Bolkosky, but he couldn't see him anywhere. Just as Hunter sat down, applause began and the first performer walked onto the stage.

♫

May sat across from Hunter in the DeBot cafeteria. She was eating a vegetable rice casserole thing and he was having a cheeseburger and french fries.

"Look!" said Hunter, pointing a french fry. "There's Selena."

May saw the same teenage girl from the Play-In putting her tray away. The girl flipped her long black hair over her shoulder and smiled so that dimples showed on her cheeks. She laughed and wrapped her arm through the arm of the boy with the spiky orange hair, and they left the cafeteria.

"Not Selena," said May, returning to her casserole.

"Selena," said Hunter.

"Not Selena," said May.

"Selena," said Hunter, "And" he emphasized what he was saying by pointing his french fry at May's face, "I found out that the teen dorms are on the fourth floor of our very own Hansen Hall."

May smiled. "The boys have the fourth floor of our dorm. The girls have the fourth floor of Neale Hall."

Hunter's face fell. "Really? How do you know?"

May shrugged. "I overheard some girls talking. You know, you could go up to our fourth floor and find the spiky haired boy and ask him if his girlfriend is Selena Montoya."

"She is not his girlfriend!" objected Hunter.

"You could spy on him anyway," said May. "It would be good practice for spying on Mr. Bolkosky."

Hunter smiled mischievously. "It might be fun. You could come with me."

May shook her head. "Girls aren't allowed on the fourth floor of Hansen Hall."

Hunter's phone rang. He pulled it out of his pocket and answered. "Yeah? ... That's OK. ... Early? I don't know. ... I guess I could try. ... OK." Hunter hung up. "That was Sebastian. He can't meet us tonight but thinks we should all get to A class early. He's going to try to think up a plan for handling Mr. Bolkosky."

May nodded. "Have you called Bayly yet?"

Hunter shook his head. "I guess I should do that. Should we invite her over or should we just tell her about getting to A class early."

"Whatever you want."

"I want to spy on spiky hair boy, so I'll just tell Bayly to meet us early."

"OK."

Tuesday

Bayly hurried toward the CCC from Baldwin Hall, the dormitory where she and her mom were sharing a room. Mrs. Hall was going to Starbucks to get coffee and muffins, but Bayly had told her just to bring the breakfast to A class.

She was the first to arrive; it wasn't even 7:45 yet, which was the time the kids had set to meet. She hoped Sebastian had come up with a good plan. Bayly had had a miserable night. Usually, when she was feeling bad, playing the violin took her mind off her problems. She had practiced for almost two hours last night, but it hadn't helped. She kept thinking about how much better everything would have sounded if she'd been playing her Goldin.

The door to the classroom opened and Sebastian, May and Mrs. Wong walked in together. Mrs. Wong walked to a chair at the side of the room, sat down and began paging through a notebook. Sebastian and May hurried to Bayly.

"Have you seen Hunter yet?" asked Sebastian.

"No," whispered Bayly. "Do you have a plan?"

"Well, sort of," answered Sebastian. "Do you remember how yesterday Hunter kind of delayed his turn by asking Mr. Bolkosky a lot of questions?"

Both girls nodded.

"Well, I thought it would seem natural if he did the same thing today. He could ask Mr. Bolkosky how many violins he had, what kinds they were, if he could have any violin in the world, what would it be . . . that kind of thing."

May was nodding.

Bayly said, "Yeah, I guess that would be something. I mean, if he stole my violin then he might act funny at Hunter's questions. It's worth a try."

The three started unpacking their violins and getting ready for their class. Bayly looked at her watch. "Where is Hunter? It's almost eight o'clock. If he doesn't get here early, he won't know what to do."

Just then her cell phone started humming.

"It's a text from Hunter," she told the others.

Bayly read her screen, and then looked at the others with a puzzled expression. "Who's spiky hair boy? And why would I care that he has a Goldin?"

May said, "Spiky hair boy is Selena Montoya's boyfriend."

Sebastian gave May a puzzled look, but Bayly was focused on texting Hunter back. Finally she snapped shut her phone. "I just told Hunter the plan. I hope he gets the message in time. What's this about spiky hair boy?"

May answered. "He's this boy in the teen dorm. Hunter was going to spy on him last night to see whether his girlfriend is Selena Montoya." This time both Bayly and Sebastian gave her puzzled looks.

"I know, it's crazy but Hunter thinks Selena Montoya is here at institute, and every time we see the girl who looks like Selena Montoya, she is with this boy who is really tall and skinny and has spiky orange hair. The girl teens are in a different dorm, but the teen boys are on the fourth floor of our dorm, so Hunter was going to spy on spiky hair boy last night as a sort of practice for spying on Mr. Bolkosky."

Bayly frowned. "Well, that makes perfect sense—not. So what's with this boy having a Goldin?"

May shrugged. "I saw him at the Play-In and he didn't have a Goldin then. If he has one now, maybe he stole yours. He seems like a better suspect than Mr. Bolkosky."

As May was talking, Hunter, Mr. Petersen, Blake and Mr. Bolkosky all walked into the classroom.

May whispered to Bayly, "Do you think he had time to get the message?"

Bayly shrugged and shook her head to show she didn't know.

"Good morning, everyone," said Mr. Bolkosky.

The violin teacher put his case on the table at the front of the room and worked at getting his stuff out and organized. Hunter put his violin on a chair right by the door and started taking it out. Bayly rushed over to him.

She whispered,"Did you get my message?"

Before Hunter could answer, Bayly's mom opened the door. "Oh, thank goodness you're right here. Take this cup, I was about to spill it." As Mrs. Hall walked into the room, Bayly had to step backward. Mrs.

Hall moved into the space between Hunter and Bayly. "Here." Bayly took the coffee cup and moved to a seat.

"What is this?" Bayly asked, sniffing the cup.

"Hazelnut steamer. Here, take your muffin too."

Bayly took the muffin and looked over at Hunter. His violin was ready and he was moving toward Mr. Bolkosky. "Can I go first today?" asked Hunter.

Great, Bayly thought. If he doesn't know the plan, there'll be no time to tell him.

"Certainly," said Mr. Bolkosky.

May and Sebastian took seats next to Bayly.

"Wow, nice shoes," said Hunter.

Sebastian, May and Bayly all looked at Mr. Bolkosky's shoes. Although he was dressed in a button shirt, jacket, and dress pants, he was wearing black converse sneakers.

"Thanks," said Mr. Bolkosky. He answered absent-mindedly, as he was still looking through some papers and wasn't totally organized yet for Hunter's lesson. The teacher put all the papers in a folder except one, which he laid on top of the folder with a pen. "OK, Hunter—"

But before Mr. Bolkosky could continue, Hunter interrupted, "How many violins do you own?"

Mr. Bolkosky smiled, "Three. And you'll have to save the rest of your questions until after your lesson this time, Hunter."

Sebastian, May and Bayly all exhaled in disappointment. Hunter hadn't been able to ask anything important.

"Can I ask you one more and you can think about it during my lesson and answer it when I'm finished?"

"If I were to spend your lesson thinking about your question, then I would be a very distracted teacher, wouldn't I?" laughed Mr. Bolkosky. "Question and answer after your lesson."

They worked on different spots in *Gigue*, especially a section that Mr. Bolkosky had asked Hunter to practice. When they were finished, they bowed to each other and Mr. Bolkosky said, "OK, Hunter, what was that question?"

Without any hesitation or embarrassment, Hunter asked, "Do you own a Goldin violin?"

Mr. Bolkosky squinted his eyes in surprise and looked directly at May. "Goodness, there seems to be quite a bit of interest in whether or not I own a Goldin. No, I don't. I wouldn't even want to. The Goldin has great sound, but the color is distracting—for me as a violinist, but even more so for an audience. I think when a performer has a Goldin, the audience is so intrigued by the glowing yellow color, that part of the musical experience is lost." He turned toward the other three kids, "Who's next?"

The students each got one-on-one time with Mr. Bolkosky who praised and prodded and helped them with their pieces. When the class was almost over, he handed May and Sebastian envelopes inviting them both to perform in the series of informal recitals on Wednesday night.

After A class, the friends did not get time to talk. Sebastian had to babysit, Hunter's dad made Hunter attend Blake's lesson, and May's mom had scheduled time in a practice room for May.

♫

Their C class was held in NFAC 212, a small concert room. The class focused on repertoire and contained about twenty-five students. The four friends stood on the stage behind the others and tried to talk.

"What do you think of Mr. Bolkosky's answer?" asked Bayly.

"I believe him," answered Hunter right away. "I don't think he wants a Goldin."

"I don't know," said May. "His answer seemed practiced. He looked right at me before he answered Hunter, like he was remembering that I asked him the same question yesterday, and he was showing me he had a better answer today."

"Well, he came up with a pretty good one, if he made it up," said Sebastian.

Bayly shook her head. "I don't know what to think. What's the deal with spiky hair boy?"

Hunter was about to answer when the C teacher started rearranging the students so everyone could see, tall students in back and short students in front. May and Sebastian were made to go to the front, Hunter ended up on the end in the middle and only Bayly stayed at the back.

After they had played *Musette*, with the new bowing, May felt a touch on her shoulder. Hunter was standing behind her, hunched down. Sebastian turned too. "Can you go swimming after class?" Hunter asked.

May and Sebastian nodded and Hunter said, "We can talk there. Bayly's coming too."

The teacher started talking about the new piece in Book 4 and how students who had made it through Book 4 before it was added should get a new Book 4 and learn that piece. When May glanced behind her she saw that Hunter had gotten back into place.

♫

Bayly put her long hair in a ponytail and grabbed her bag which contained a towel, shampoo and the clothes she had just changed out of. In the pool area, she found her mom sitting on bleachers off to the side. She put the bag down on the empty seat in front of her mom. Mrs. Hall was talking to a woman Bayly didn't recognize. "Mom?" said Bayly. "Here's my stuff." Mrs. Hall nodded but didn't interrupt her conversation. Bayly turned toward the pool and saw her friends. May and a girl with blond hair, a few years younger than Bayly, were sitting on the side of the pool, kicking their legs into the water and talking. Sebastian and Hunter were standing and tussling at the water's edge. A whistle sounded from the lifeguard, but it was too late. Hunter had pushed Sebastian into the water.

The lifeguard admonished Hunter. "No rough housing!"

Sebastian's head came up out of the water.

"Sorry!" Hunter yelled to the life guard.

Sebastian heard Hunter and said, "That's OK," as if Hunter had been apologizing to him.

Bayly grabbed Hunter's arm and pulled him to a sitting position beside the girls. Sebastian climbed out of the pool and sat next to Hunter.

"I went to Harry's after A class, but nobody knew anything more about my Goldin," Bayly said. "So tell me about this spiky hair boy."

Hunter nodded. "I started spying on him last night. I found that from the stairwell, I could see when he went in and out of his room. I had my violin with me, so if anybody else came up the stairs I could start playing—like I was practicing somewhere where I wouldn't bother anyone." The kids all nodded. Practicing in stairwells was common at institute. "So, I watched for a long time last night and he went in and out a bunch, but he didn't shower and neither did his roommate."

Bayly started to interrupt, but Hunter held up his hand to tell her to be quiet.

"I figured since they didn't shower last night, they would shower this morning. So, I got up early and stood at the stairwell and watched their door. Sure enough, they both got up around 7:00 and went to the bathroom and left their door unlocked."

May gasped, "You didn't!"

Hunter shrugged. "It wasn't like I was going to steal anything. I just wanted to look around."

Sebastian was shaking his head, his sister giggled, and Bayly said, "So, go on. What did you see?"

"Well, remember, I was looking for evidence that he knew Selena Montoya. I wasn't thinking about your Goldin at all. His room was really messy, with clothes on the floor and all sorts of papers and scores on the desks. I glanced around, but it all seemed like institute or music stuff. Then I thought about how some people put pictures and stuff in their violin cases. So, I opened the violin case that was in the corner, but there was nothing in it. I figured I'd have to leave soon, but then I thought I'd look quick under his bed. There was another violin case under the bed, so I pulled it out and opened it. No pictures, but it was a Goldin."

"Are you sure?" asked Bayly.

Hunter looked offended. "It was glowing yellow. It was a Goldin."

"Maybe it was his roommate's," said Sebastian.

Hunter shook his head. "His roommate is a cellist. I saw him practicing last night."

The 1812 Overture rang out from the bleachers. Bayly looked, but her mom wasn't sitting on the bleachers anymore. She climbed out the of pool and hurried over to her mom's bag. Reaching inside, Bayly pulled out the phone just as it stopped ringing. She started to open it and check who had called, but Mrs. Hall arrived just then.

"Where were you? You got a call," said Bayly.

"I went to the bathroom," said Mrs. Hall. Bayly's mom took the phone and listened to her message.

"Was it Dad?" asked Bayly.

Mrs. Hall was shaking her head and then she closed the phone. "No, it was that same wrong number as yesterday."

"Well, if Dad calls will you let me talk to him?" asked Bayly.

"Of course."

Bayly turned back to her friends but only Sebastian sat at the side of the pool. She looked around and saw everyone else lined up to go on the high dive. Bayly walked over to Sebastian.

"Aren't you going to go?" She pointed with her arm at the high dive and May, Sebastian and Rachel.

He shook his head.

Bayly sat down next to him. "I'll go if you go."

Sebastian smiled. "Then I guess you won't be going."

"Ah, come on, what could happen?" Bayly asked.

"I could die," said Sebastian, "or worse, make myself look like an idiot."

"Haven't you ever given a recital?" asked Bayly.

"That's totally different," said Sebastian.

"Not really. I was so terrified at my first recital. You guys all started really young, so you probably don't even remember your first recital. But I was almost eight. I remember thinking how everyone else had done this before and it was easy for them, but that I was going to get up there and panic and not remember a single note of my piece, or maybe trip walking in front of everyone, or I'd drop my bow and it would break. I imagined all sorts of awful things happening."

"How'd it go?" asked Sebastian.

"Well, I didn't trip, and I didn't forget every note, but I did mess up in two places. But, to be honest, I didn't care that much. Everyone applauded, and then it was over. And, it hadn't been as hard as I thought it would be."

Sebastian didn't look at Bayly. Instead he stared out at his legs, which looked pale and distorted by the water.

"So, what do you say?" Bayly continued. "Go on the high dive?"

Sebastian frowned and turned his head sideways at her. "Let me think about it. Maybe tomorrow."

Bayly smiled and put her hand on his back gently. "That a boy." Then she pushed hard and shoved him into the water.

May liked her B class because it concerned technique. Today the teacher was focusing on dynamics and teaching the students the Italian words used in music to describe how a piece should be played. May thought the words were beautiful: *pizzicato*, *pianissimo*, *allegretto*, *legato*.

The teacher would say an Italian word and ask if anyone knew what it meant. There were twelve students, and usually somebody knew. Then she'd ask everyone if they could name a piece that had that Italian direction. If someone did, she would talk about the place in the piece where the direction was written, and they'd practice it. If nobody could name a piece, she would write the word on the board and move on.

At the end of the class, the teacher added to the list of Italian words on the chalkboard and told each student to pick one word, find out what it meant and be ready to name a piece that featured that direction for class on Wednesday.

May wrote down *dolce*. She'd heard the word before but wasn't sure what it meant.

As she was putting her stuff away, Hunter walked up. "Want to go to the institute store? I'm going to get my t-shirt and see what else they have."

"Sure," answered May.

May and her mom followed Hunter and his dad and brother to the room in the NFAC that served as the institute store. There were t-shirts, mugs, recordings, books, pencils, bow friends, and even stuffed animals playing instruments. Mrs. Wong loved books and went straight to them. There were so many to choose from. She leafed through *Math Vitamins*, a book of math games for young children; saw *Nurtured by Love* by Shinichi Suzuki, which she already owned; closely examined a collection of Suzuki duets; and kept moving through the selection of books.

May picked up a Koala bear that had arms that one could pinch open and shut so that it could hold on to things.

"Look at these," said Blake. He was holding up a little plastic worm that could snap onto a bow. May looked at the box below Blake's hand. It held all sorts of plastic bow creatures in bright colors.

"Oh! I love these," she said, grabbing a pink butterfly and a white ghost.

"May, come over here," said Mrs. Wong. She had found the Suzuki books and recordings and was holding up Book 4. "We should get you the new version with the extra piece, so you can learn it."

"OK," said May without much enthusiasm. "Can I have one of these bow creatures?" She held up the pink butterfly.

"How much are they?"

"I don't know. I'll check."

The two families roamed around the store looking at all that was available. Hunter, Blake and Mr. Petersen each got a purple institute t-shirt. May got the new music and recording for Book 4, and a white sunhat with a large floppy brim and black violins all over it. Mrs. Wong bought two, commenting on how hot it had been and how the hats would keep the sun off their faces.

On the way to the dormitory to put their things away before dinner, Blake rode his scooter ahead of everyone else. Mr. Petersen and Mrs. Wong discussed the evening schedule, trying to decide which events to attend.

Hunter walked next to May. "I haven't seen spiky hair boy or Selena all day, have you?"

May shook her head.

Hunter said, "Maybe they'll be at DeBot for dinner."

May nodded absentmindedly.

"I want you to do something for me," said Hunter. "I want you to spy on Selena and find out if she's really Selena."

May frowned. "Why don't you just go and ask her for her autograph? If she's Selena you'll find out and get her autograph, and if she's not . . . " May trailed off, not really sure what would happen if she were not Selena.

"Well, that's it, isn't it?" said Hunter. "If she's not Selena, I'll look stupid."

"I thought you were totally sure she's Selena," said May.

"Well, I'm not," said Hunter. "Please will you spy on her for me?"

May sighed. "Really, I would. But the thing is my mom keeps pretty good track of me. I can't just tell her that I'm going to spy on somebody."

"Wait, I have an idea," said Hunter, taking out his cell phone and punching the numbers.

"Bayly," he said into the phone. "Can we come to your room after dinner and play cards or something? . . . Great. Call us when you get back."

Hunter put away his phone.

"She's going to call us when she gets back from dinner. They're going to a restaurant downtown or something. And guess what? Neale Hall, with the teen girls, is on the way to Baldwin Hall where Bayly is staying. We could walk through Neale on the way to Baldwin." Hunter was lifting his eyebrows up and down to make sure May understood and agreed.

She laughed. "I'll check with my mom, but she'll probably be OK with it. She wants to go to the faculty recital tonight anyway. But I'm not going into Selena's room. I'll just walk up and down the hall or something. Or maybe I can ask someone at the front desk about her."

♫

The ice cream at the DeBot dining center was really good. May and Hunter were both getting second helpings. Mr. Petersen and Mrs. Wong had left the cafeteria to get ready for the recital. Blake was going swimming with a friend and his parents.

Selena and spiky hair boy had not had dinner in DeBot, as far as Hunter and May could tell, but they thought they'd stay in the cafeteria as long as they could just to make sure. When they were nearly the last people there, Hunter and May stood up, put away their trays and headed back to Hansen Hall.

"Let's stop by my room and get a deck of cards," said Hunter.

After he had grabbed the cards, they headed to the door that would put them right across from Neale Hall. Before they opened the door, May said, "Hey look! There they are."

The two friends stayed inside and looked out the glass door. Neale Hall was a short distance from Hansen Hall. A sidewalk connected them, with grassy areas on either side and other sidewalks heading toward campus and DeBot. The Neale Hall door straight across from them had bushes on both sides. Behind one of the bushes were two girls, including the Selena girl. The other was short and had purple hair. They were pushing each other and giggling. All in an instant, they were quiet and didn't move. Frozen, their hiding place was pretty good. Hunter could see two teen boys walking down one of the sidewalks, talking, and not paying any attention to the girls.

Suddenly the two girls jumped out, holding yellow and orange guns. They sprayed streams of water at the boys. The girl with the purple hair soaked the blue t-shirt of one of the boys. The Selena girl got her target in the back of the head, although a lot of the water missed him. Before the boys knew what happened, the two teen girls opened the door to Neale Hall and disappeared inside.

The teen boys darted for the door and followed the girls.

"Come on," said Hunter, grabbing May's hand and pulling her out the door. They ran the short distance to Neale Hall and went in the same door as the teens. The door opened in a stairwell, and they could hear pounding feet and voices from above. Hunter and May rushed up the stairs. When they got to the third floor, they passed the teen boys coming down. May and Hunter paused just above them and listened.

"—stay up there all night now. We'll have to wait until morning to get them," said one of the boys.

"They won't stay there all night. I think we should go back and fill up the balloons. It's only seven o'clock. There's no way they'll stay in there all night."

The voices of the teen boys faded as they made it down to the ground level and exited the building.

"Now's your chance," said Hunter. "Go up to the fourth floor and spy on her. We know she's there."

Faced with having to really do it, May didn't want to, but she also didn't want to disappoint Hunter. She stood frozen in place, a nervous look on her face.

"Come on," said Hunter. "You promised."

"What should I do? Everyone's going to know I don't belong there, even if I am a girl."

"Say you need to use the bathroom," said Hunter, thinking quickly. "Say the one downstairs is closed for cleaning or something. You don't have to be there very long. Just quick enough to see her name tag."

May nodded and nervously started walking up the steps to the fourth floor. She didn't think anyone would be cleaning a bathroom at seven o'clock at night, but maybe the girls wouldn't pay her too much attention.

She opened the door to the fourth floor hall and hesitantly stepped in on the carpet. A Taylor Swift song was coming from an open door on her left. She took several slow steps down the hall, looking into the room with the open door on her left. Suddenly, she was bumped from behind by girls leaving a door on her right.

"Sorry," someone said. It wasn't the Selena girl or the girl with purple hair. This girl had long blonde hair, wore eyeliner, blue eye shadow and deep red lipstick and did a double take when she saw May. "Can I help you?"

"Um. I... I... I" stuttered May, "I need to use the bathroom. The one downstairs is closed."

The blonde girl pointed down the hall, and May hurried in that direction.

The moment she opened the door, she saw the Selena girl and purple hair girl. They were standing by the sinks, filling up their water guns. Their backs were toward May, but she could see their faces, bent over the sinks, in the reflection of the mirrors. Neither of them was wearing a name tag. May hurried to a stall and closed the door. They hadn't seemed to notice her. May sat on the toilet and listened.

"I think we should sneak into Hansen and hide out on one of the lower floors," said one of the girls. May wasn't sure which voice belonged to which girl and she could no longer see them. "They'll never suspect that. We can watch from inside and get them when they come down the stairs."

"I don't know how we can get there without them seeing us," said the other girl. "They've got to be watching all the doors by now."

"Where's Tony? Maybe he could help."

"He's rehearsing for Thursday's recital. Besides, I don't trust him either. He's just as likely to soak us as any of the other boys."

The two teens were quiet. May was thinking fast, trying to come up with a plan.

She stepped out from the stall. "I could help you," she said nervously, having a hard time believing she could be so brave.

"Who are you?" asked the Selena girl.

"I'm May. I'm staying in Hansen Hall. I was visiting a friend here. I have an idea for sneaking you into my dorm." She told the girls her plan and they agreed. May darted out of the bathroom and back to the stairwell. Hunter was sitting on the third floor landing.

"Come on, hurry," said May running past him.

"What's going on? What did you find out?"

"We're going to help the Selena girl and the purple hair girl sneak into our dorm."

"Is she really Selena Montoya?" asked Hunter.

"I don't know," said May, pushing open the Neale Hall door and heading to Hansen Hall. "I just thought if we helped them, then maybe we could learn something."

They climbed the stairs to their floor. "Grab your new t-shirt and your dad's new t-shirt. I'm going to get those sunhats my mom bought today." When they had the stuff, they returned to Neale Hall. Hunter stayed in the stairwell while May took the clothing to the fourth floor. When she returned, she was with the two teen girls. They were each wearing a purple institute t-shirt and a floppy sunhat. It was hard to tell who they were.

Before they opened the door to leave the building, the Selena girl turned to May and Hunter. "We need to act like we're all really good friends. Like we are kids your age, staying in the dorm with you."

May thought it could work. Neither girl was very tall. In fact Bayly was probably taller than both of them.

Hunter said, "Do you ever watch *A Girl in the City*? We could talk about it." May stifled a giggle. That was Selena Montoya's television show.

"Perfect," said the Selena girl, not batting an eye. "Let's go."

The Selena girl and Hunter walked next to each other and May and purple hair girl walked next to each other. Purple hair girl said, "This is so great of you. The boys will have no idea what happened."

May said, "We saw you with the water guns earlier, and it looked like fun."

"It's been so hot," said the purple hair girl. "It seemed like the perfect idea. We got the guns at Kmart which is just across the street."

"Oh," said May, looking around, afraid that someone would jump out and shoot her with a water gun or throw a water balloon at her.

"Is this your first year at institute?" asked purple hair girl holding the door to Hansen Hall open for her.

"Yeah. Is it yours?"

"No. I've been coming since I was about your age. How old are you?"

"Twelve," answered May.

"Oh. I thought you were younger. Hey, next year you could come to the teen dorm. It's really a lot of fun."

"It looks like fun," said May.

They all started walking up the stairs. It hadn't been hard at all to fool the boys. When they got to the second level, Hunter opened the door to the second floor and everyone stepped inside. When the door was shut, the Selena girl said, "Hey, thanks a lot, you guys. We owe you."

Hunter had his mouth open to say something but purple hair girl who had been looking through the door window into the stairwell said, "There they are."

She and the Selena girl disappeared into the stairwell. As the door shut, Hunter grabbed it and dashed through. May followed. They could hear laughter and voices from below. They went down the stairs but nobody was at the bottom. Hunter opened the door to the outside just in time to see the two teen girls and two teen boys running down the grassy area behind DeBot and toward the outdoor sports complex.

"Did you find out?" asked May.

Hunter shook his head. "I talked about the television show and how much I like Selena Montoya and think she's a great actress, but the girl wasn't really paying attention. She was distracted, looking for the teen boys I guess."

"You should've just asked her," said May. "How could she say, 'Oh, you like Selena Montoya? Well that's me!' She'd have to do something like pretend she wasn't listening. What else could she do without looking all arrogant and stuff?"

Hunter's face brightened. "She really looks like Selena. Do you think she is? That I just said the wrong things?"

May hesitated. She didn't think the Selena girl was Selena, but she didn't want to disappoint Hunter. And really, it was possible. "Well, I don't know. I'm just saying if she was Selena, she'd have a hard time talking to you with what you were saying."

"Well, didn't you ask her friend?" Hunter said. "What were you two talking about?"

May had been so nervous about everything that she had totally forgotten to try to get information about Selena from purple hair girl. "I'm sorry. I didn't find anything out. We just talked about institute and stuff. But, you know, when they bring back the t-shirts and hats we can try to find out again."

Hunter beamed. "I forgot about that."

His cell phone rang. It was Bayly asking where they were. They went to her room and played cards until bedtime. When they returned to their rooms, they discovered that their t-shirts and hats had been returned while they were gone.

"How did they know where to return them?" Hunter asked his dad.

Mr. Petersen shrugged. “I don’t know. I guess they asked around.”

Before she shut the door May said, “Don’t worry. We’ll figure out something else to solve the mystery.”

Wednesday

"I thought I'd start our class today with a little demonstration," said Mr. Bolkosky turning around and opening a violin case.

Sebastian sat with the others in the front row of chairs and yawned. His family had gone to the faculty recital last night, and then out for ice cream at Emy J's afterward. They hadn't gotten home until almost 9:00, which was late by Phelps family standards. Greg and Lucy had been whining and wouldn't go to bed right away. Sebastian had gotten into a fight with Rachel about what to wear for the talent show tonight. He wished he'd gotten a few more hours of sleep.

When Mr. Bolkosky turned around, he was holding a Goldin violin.

Four mouths gaped.

"Where did you get that?" asked Bayly first. "I thought you said you didn't have or want a Goldin."

Mr. Bolkosky smiled a sly smile. "What? Do you think I might have stolen it from Harry's?"

The four mouths that had just closed gaped again.

Mr. Bolkosky laughed. "It's no secret that a Goldin was stolen from Harry's this week. And, truly, it was some very fine deduction by May, am I right? Did you see me playing this in the practice rooms on Monday?"

May nodded but couldn't say anything.

Hunter looked confused. "So you did steal it?"

Mr. Bolkosky laughed again. "I didn't steal this, and it isn't mine. One of my home students, Peter, ordered it from Augustina Goldin several months ago and arranged for Mr. Harry to bring it here. Peter was supposed to come to institute but broke his arm this summer. I offered to pick up the violin, check it out, and take it to him."

Bayly said, "But that's what we did. We ordered a violin from Augustina Goldin in the spring and Mr. Harry was going to bring it to institute for us to pick up. In fact, I played it and everything before it was stolen."

"Ah," said Mr. Bolkosky, "so it was *your* Goldin. No wonder you are all so interested in it. Have you heard anything about what happened to it?" As he asked the question, Mr. Bolkosky looked at Mrs. Hall.

She shook her head. "No clues at all. I'm not sure anyone will ever know what happened. It was insured, so Mr. Harry won't lose any money. Bayly will just have to wait until Augustina can build another Goldin.

Mr. Bolkosky held his student's Goldin out toward Bayly. "Would you like to play this one today?"

Bayly's eyes lit up. "Can I?"

"I talked to Peter last night and he said you all could use it during today's class, if you want. I know it is a little large for some of you. He did ask me to make sure you are careful."

Bayly played *La Folia.* The tone was rich and clean, noticeably better than her backup violin. Sebastian experimented by listening with his eyes open and listening with his eyes closed. He wasn't sure whether the yellow glow of the violin was distracting or not.

Hunter went next and played some warm up scales on the Goldin violin, but Mr. Petersen spoke up after that and requested that Hunter do the rest of his lesson on his regular violin. May and Sebastian also did some scales with the Goldin, but their lessons with their regular violins. May was nervous to hold such an expensive violin and was relieved when she could hand it back to Mr. Bolkosky. Sebastian experimented by playing one scale, eyes open and looking at his bow, and one scale eyes closed, and decided that the violin's color was distracting, but then so was its size.

♫

After C class, Bayly asked Sebastian if he was going to go off the high dive today.

"No, in fact, I can't go swimming at all today."

"Why not?" asked Bayly.

"I have to go home for lunch," Sebastian answered. He paused and then continued, "My family's doing something in the talent show tonight and it'll be our last chance to practice."

Bayly's eyes lit up. "You're in the talent show? What're you going to do?"

Sebastian shook his head and said. "You'll just have to wait and see. It's pretty hokey. Don't laugh, OK?"

Bayly smiled broadly. "I don't think I can promise that. Is it supposed to be funny?"

"I don't know. Not really. Maybe a little."

"Now I'm excited. Funny, but not funny. Is it musical or a skit?"

"You'll just have to wait," answered Sebastian, smiling now.

"OK. Do you know where your informal recital is going to be?" asked Bayly.

"I don't have the room number with me, but it's in the CCC."

"Bring it to orchestra," said Bayly. "I'm going to try to watch both you and May."

"Great. See you at orchestra," said Sebastian.

♫

Hunter stuck his head in May's room where she was sitting on her bed, writing on the back of a postcard, with other postcards, paper and pens spread out around her.

"Aren't you getting ready to go swimming?"

May shook her head. "Sebastian had to go home, and Bayly and her mom drove to Plover to have lunch and do some shopping, so I thought I'd skip swimming today."

Hunter made an exaggerated expression, pretending to be hurt. "What? If it is just me, then you don't want to go swimming?"

Misunderstanding Hunter's joke, May immediately felt bad. "Oh, no, Hunter. It isn't that. I haven't written any postcards since I've been here, and I promised my friends I'd write them. I really need to get some practice time in too."

"Can I see?" asked Hunter, sitting on the bed and picking up a postcard.

May held the postcard she was writing to her chest. "Of course not," she said. "These are private."

The postcard Hunter had grabbed was empty of writing. He looked at the picture side which showed some of the buildings on campus and had a cartoon of the UWSP mascot, Stevie Pointer, and then put the card back down on the bed. "Postcards aren't really private, you know. Anyone can read them. In the post office sorting room, the mail men probably pass around really good postcards."

May giggled, imagining a bunch of old men reading her card. "Well, still, I don't want you to read mine."

"OK." Hunter stood. "You know, I should practice too. I'll go back to my room and work on some things. If you want to go outside later and see if anyone is playing music on the lawn, let me know."

"Sure," said May. "I wanted to do that too. I love the way people just gather together outside and start playing together. It's so fun. On one hand, it makes perfect sense that we all know the same pieces since we are all Suzuki students; on the other hand, it seems really weird, like we are on some different planet."

Hunter nodded. "I know. Don't go down without me."

"OK."

A few minutes later, May could hear the notes of *Gigue* dancing across the hall.

After she finished writing her postcards, May got out her violin and practiced her Handel Sonata several times. May had been invited by Mr. Bolkosky to perform in an informal recital tonight. Her mom had asked another mom about it and found out that there were a whole lot of informal recitals all scheduled at the same time in different classrooms around campus. Each recital featured about seven or eight students playing pieces of varying levels. The performers got a little dressed up, if they had dress clothes. May had brought two dresses, neither very fancy, and thought she'd wear the pink one tonight. She'd save the blue one for the final Friday night concert.

May was proud to be chosen to perform. Not every student was, but she almost wished she hadn't been. Performing made her so nervous. Would it be easier to perform in front of institute people or more difficult? When she thought about it, it seemed like it could go either way. Suzuki kids all knew how stressful and scary it was to perform, but then again they also knew all the pieces and if she made any mistake at all, someone would notice.

After running through the Sonata one more time, May left her room and knocked on Hunter's door. She could hear him playing one of their orchestra pieces. The sound of his violin stopped and the door opened. May saw Mr. Petersen lying on one bed with a book on his chest and his eyes closed. Could he really sleep while Hunter practiced? Through the wall she could hear Blake playing *Seitz 2:3*.

"Ready to go outside?" asked May.

"Just a minute," said Hunter. "Would you come in

and play this part with me? I keep getting confused at the key change."

"Sure," said May.

♫

After orchestra, Sebastian said he had to hurry home but he wished May good luck on her recital. "My sister Lucy is in your recital too, but our recitals are in different buildings so I probably won't get to see you perform."

May said, "How do you know your sister is in my recital?"

"It's all posted on tables in the NFAC courtyard."

"Oh," said May.

Hunter turned to May. "If Selena Montoya is here, she might be in one of the informal recitals. I'm going to go down and look at the lists and see if her name is there. Want to come?"

May shook her head. "I'd like to, but Mama and I are going to one of the lectures. It's about careers as a music educator. I'm sort of thinking about being a music teacher in a school, but I'm not sure, so I wanted to go and hear what they had to say."

Bayly stood up and walked toward Hunter. "I'll go with you. I want to see the lists too. I have a couple of friends from last year that I haven't seen and I want to see if their names are there."

"Great," said Hunter.

"See you later," said May.

Hunter and Bayly walked down the stairs to where the recital lists were posted. Hunter didn't find Selena

Montoya's name on the list of performers for the informal recitals. Still, it wasn't wasted effort as Hunter wrote down the three different recitals he wanted to attend. His brother Blake was playing a Seitz piece in the CCC, Sebastian was playing *La Folia* in the CCC, and May was playing the Handel Sonata in the NFAC. Hunter figured he would be able to see Blake, and then run across the parking lot to the NFAC and see May's recital if he hurried.

Bayly didn't find any of the names of the friends she was looking for on the recital list, but she did see one friend's little sister's name. The little sister's recital was in a room down the hall from Sebastian's recital. Hunter and Bayly talked about it, and Bayly said she'd go to support Sebastian if Hunter promised to go to May's recital. The way Bayly said it was like she thought Hunter might not show up. He couldn't understand why she would think that. Hunter really liked May and wouldn't miss her recital for anything.

When Blake played the last note of his piece, Mr. Petersen took a picture and the flash lit Blake's face. Hunter clapped loudly and whooped a little. When Blake straightened from his bow he had a crooked smile on his face and he was looking at his cheering older brother. When he returned to the seat between Hunter and Mr. Petersen, Hunter said, "Great job, Blake. I've gotta move fast to see May's recital."

As he stood to head toward the door at the back of the room, Mr. Petersen said, "Meet us at the talent show."

Hunter nodded and took off running. The most direct route to the NFAC was through the parking lot. Hunter jogged carefully, making sure none of the cars would back up and hit him. He went in the doors by the Suzuki office and up the nearest stairwell. Someone must have just entered the stairwell because he could hear the loud clomp of feet on the cement steps. Looking up, Hunter saw spiky hair boy and spiky hair boy's roommate heading up the stairs. Hunter slowed his pace, stepped softly, and listened to their conversation. He didn't think they knew he was behind them.

Spiky hair boy said, "Are you sure nobody saw you?"

The roommate answered, "I was careful. Don't be so worried."

"Well, give it to me then."

The roommate made a grunt of disgust. "I didn't bring it with me. It's in the room under your bed. You can have it when we get back."

"But I already gave you the money."

"I said it's under your bed," said the roommate.

The two teens had reached the second floor, which was where May's recital was, and were climbing the stairs to the third floor.

Hunter paused on the landing. If he followed them, would he be able to figure out what they were talking about? It sounded like spiky hair boy's roommate had stolen something, maybe the Goldin. Hunter looked up at the backs of the teens and then exited the stairwell. May's recital was in one of the orchestra rooms close by. He pulled open the door to the recital, releasing the deep notes of a cello. Hunter saw a boy about the age of Blake playing. He hoped May hadn't gone yet. Hunter waited until the boy had finished before walking in and slipping into a seat by Mrs. Wong.

"I didn't miss her, did I?" asked Hunter.

"No," said Mrs. Wong. "She's after the next performer." Mrs. Wong pointed at the front row. "May's sitting up front by Sebastian's sisters." Hunter recognized Rachel from swimming. The other girl was only about four or five.

"Which one performed?" asked Hunter.

"The little one," said Mrs. Wong. "She played the viola. Oh, it was so cute."

They stopped talking and applauded as the next performer walked out in front.

He was a fairly young boy playing the unaccompanied Bach *Gavotte*, popularly called UBG. At one point, he started in on the wrong section but caught himself and backed up and then played the right section. When he took his bow, Hunter could tell how angry he was at himself. Hunter felt bad for him, but then thought that it probably took some of the pressure off May. If someone else in the recital messes up before you, then you don't feel the pressure to be perfect yourself.

Of course, May was perfect. She played the Sonata like she'd written it herself. When she held her bow over her violin after her last note, Hunter clapped loudly and whooped until someone in front of him turned around. Hunter just laughed. May waved and started to sit next to Sebastian's sisters but then moved back to where her mom and Hunter were sitting. Mrs. Wong slid the case out from under her chair, and May set the violin loosely on top.

"Great job!" said Hunter.

"Thanks," said May.

They had to be quiet as the next performer was already walking out. After that girl there was one more performer, a teen boy with braces. Just before he started, spiky hair boy, spiky hair boy's roommate, girl with purple hair and Selena Montoya all slipped into the room. They sat in seats in the front.

Hunter whispered to May, "Remind me to tell you something about spiky hair boy later."

The boy with braces played Corelli's *Courant.* His vibrato was the most vibrant Hunter had ever heard, and his long low notes were almost crying they were so sad. Hunter heard May exhale when it was over as though she'd held her breath the whole time. They both applauded, although Hunter did not whoop.

"That was amazing," said May. "Why aren't you whooping?"

"I only whoop for people I know and like."

May turned to pick up her violin case so Hunter wouldn't see her blush.

"Are you ready for the talent show?" asked Hunter as they started to leave.

May looked from her mom to Hunter. "Do you think I have time to take my violin back to my room?"

"Oh, sure," said Hunter.

At the same time, Mrs. Wong took the case from May's hand, saying "I want to put away the video camera, so I can take your violin too. Here," Mrs. Wong handed May some dollar bills. "Get yourself a soda or candy bar or something for the show. I haven't decided whether to go to the talent show or to rest and read a little."

"Sebastian's family is performing," said May.

Mrs. Wong nodded but didn't look like that fact helped her to make up her mind. "If you don't see me there, just meet me back at the room."

When they got to the gym where the talent show would be held, people were still setting up. May and Hunter roamed the hallways a little until they found some soda and candy machines.

"I'm not really hungry," said May. "Want a soda?"

"Sure," said Hunter.

May bought an orange soda for herself and a root beer for Hunter. They went outside and sat on the hill overlooking Fourth Street. Hunter told May what he had overheard between the two teen boys when he had been running from Blake's recital to May's.

"It does sound suspicious," said May. "But, really, they could be talking about lots of things."

"It seemed like they didn't want other people to know," said Hunter.

"Well, it could have been about food they weren't supposed to have or maybe they were playing a trick on another teen or maybe it was more water guns. It might not have anything to do with the Goldin."

"But I saw the Goldin under his bed and the roommate said 'it' was there."

May shrugged. "I don't know if anyone is going to figure out what happened to Bayly's Goldin. Did you hear Mrs. Hall in A class today? It sounds like everyone has just given up."

"All the more reason for us to solve the mystery."

"But how can we solve it?" asked May.

"I'm not sure," answered Hunter.

When they'd finished their sodas they went back into the gym. Things were more organized and people were starting to get seated. A giant fan had been placed near the doors to blow the cool evening air into the hot and stuffy gym. Hunter stood in front of the fan so his hair was blown straight back. He tried talking to May and his voice came out distorted by the wind. May stood in the strong breeze for a minute too. Her cheeks felt like they were being pulled back toward her ears. She laughed and the sound was wobbly and strange.

Hunter and May chose seats near the middle and Bayly and Mrs. Hall soon joined them. A few minutes later, Hunter waved at Mr. Petersen and Blake. Blake sat with his own friends and Mr. Petersen sat with some other dads.

"Where's Sebastian?" asked May.

"The performers all sit over there, off stage" said Bayly pointing to the left of the stage. "Oh, I almost forgot, will you save my seat? I'm going to go up for the days-in-a-row club."

Before the talent show began, there were awards for kids who had practiced so many days in a row. First the kids who had practiced for 100 days in a row without missing a day walked across the stage. They said their names, their ages, and what instrument they played and got a certificate.

May leaned toward Hunter. "I haven't ever kept track, but I've probably done 100 days in a row."

Next were the kids who had practiced 200 days in a row, then a whole year, then two whole years, then three years. Bayly walked across the stage for five years. The most days in a row was a teen girl who had practiced every day for thirteen years. She was sixteen years old.

May was shocked. "Can you imagine?" said May.

"Better her than me," said Hunter.

As soon as Bayly sat down in her seat, her mom's cell phone started humming. Mrs. Hall opened the phone and started listening as she worked her way out of the row of chairs and to the back of the gym.

"This is Sandra Hall. Well, yes I have, but there must be some mistake. Uh-huh–" Mrs. Hall hurried to the doors as Mr. Durbin, the MC of the talent show introduced the first act.

"We are going to start out tonight with Kayla Dean. She is four years old, plays the violin, likes dancing, teddy bears and strawberry ice cream. She will be singing 'Over the Rainbow.' "

He left the stage and a little girl, who didn't seem to be afraid of the crowd at all, walked out. She was wearing Care Bear pajamas that had rainbows all over them. Holding the microphone in one hand, she waited as the recorded music began. Then she started to sing. For being so young, her voice was powerful and clear. She belted out the tune almost better than Judy Garland.

"That was amazing," said May, applauding loudly when the girl had finished.

Hunter whooped. "I don't know her, but I'm going to whoop anyway." Then he whooped some more.

As the next act got ready, Mr. Durbin did some yo-yo tricks, including one where the yo-yo flew through the air and landed in his pocket. Then a teen girl and one of the younger female Suzuki teachers walked out on the stage, wearing sunglasses and acting very serious. They held violins and hula-hoops. They both started the hula hoops spinning around their waists and then they started playing the Bach double while hula hooping. At the places where each performer had to rest, they held the violins in a high rest position to not interfere with the spinning hula hoops. The two made it through the piece without once messing up—with their music or their hula hoops.

While the crowd roared its applause, Bayly leaned over Hunter to say to May, "We should try something like that for next year."

May's eyes got big. "No way. I don't hula hoop at all."

Bayly laughed.

Next Mr. Durbin made some amazing noises on his violin: whale, cockroach, duck, pig, cow, ambulance (both American and European), race cars, ghosts and more.

Sebastian's family was next. They were all wearing brightly colored Hawaiian shirts. Sebastian carried a boogie board, Rachel had a tambourine, Lucy had a beach ball, Mrs. Phelps carried Greg, Mr. Phelps wore a guitar strapped over his shoulder, and T.J. wasn't carrying anything, but went straight to the microphone stand and took the microphone off it.

Sebastian put his boogie board down on the stage. Greg walked over and stood on it. Sebastian held the little boy's hands up and sort of wobbled him around to look like he was surfing on the boogie board. Mrs. Phelps and Lucy passed the beach ball back and forth. T.J. turned to his dad and nodded. Mr. Phelps began playing the guitar and Rachel kept rhythm on the tambourine.

The song was "Surfin' Safari" and T.J. had the melody.

> Early in the morning we'll be starting out.
> Some honeys will be coming along.
> We're loading up the woody with the boards inside
> And heading out singing our song.

Although he was only eight, T.J.'s voice was fairly low and confident and he sang with the exact lilt of the original singer from the Beach Boys. Sebastian's little brother was a ham, belting out the words and dancing around the stage.

Everyone else in the family sang backup and different harmonies. Joining in on the main line,

> Let's go surfing now.
> Everybody's learning how.
> Come on and safari with me.

They were amazing. As the song went on, the crowd started clapping to Rachel's beat and everyone sang the refrain. The whole gym rocked. When the song was over, Hunter, Bayly and May all whooped, clapping and jumping up and down.

During the next act, a boy who could head a soccer ball twenty-five times without letting it hit the floor, Sebastian joined his friends in the audience. He sat next to Bayly, who messed up his hair.

"That was amazing," she told him. "I can't believe you said it was going to be hokey. Your family is so cool."

Sebastian's face was red, but everyone could tell he was happy. "It went better than I expected. When you practice at home, with just your family, you don't really know. It seemed like it might be embarrassing."

"No way, embarrassing," said Bayly. "I wish I had a family like that."

May leaned across Hunter, "I really liked it," she said.

Hunter was nodding enthusiastically. "Great harmony."

The rest of the talent show was good, but nothing topped Sebastian's family.

Thursday

Bayly woke to the sound of a door being shut. She opened her eyes and saw her mom entering their room, carrying a cardboard tray with two paper coffee cups and a small white paper bag.

Bayly sat up in bed rubbing her eyes. "What time is it?"

"Oh, it's early yet. I woke and couldn't sleep so I thought I'd go ahead and get breakfast." She opened the bag, took out two napkins and put a blueberry muffin on each. "Hungry?"

Bayly grimaced, "No."

"Why don't you go ahead and shower, and then maybe you'll be able to eat." Mrs. Hall took a deep breath, sighed and smiled. "It looks like it is going to be a beautiful day."

As Bayly showered, she wondered what was up with her mom. She had acted a little strange last night at the talent show, but this morning was unbelievable. Bayly's mom was not a morning person. Usually, she dragged herself out of bed rumpled and grumpy. Bayly usually tried to avoid her until she'd had her coffee and became a more pleasant person.

Bayly could understand the old mom better than the new. The shower only slightly helped to wake Bayly and she found herself dragging. So many late nights and early mornings were starting to catch up with her.

♫

The same was true in the Petersen rooms. Perfect Blake was throwing a near-tantrum. He didn't see why he had to go to Hunter's A class when he could stay in bed and sleep an extra hour. His first class wasn't until nine o'clock. Mr. Petersen stuck to his rule. The only reason to miss a brother's class was a conflict with another class. Hunter attended all of Blake's classes and Blake would attend all of Hunter's classes. There was a lot to be learned doing this, and it was special family time together.

Blake moaned and groaned but eventually got himself up and dressed.

♫

At Sebastian's house, the parents had planned for the onset of fatigue. Greg was still sleeping when Sebastian, Rachel, T.J, and Lucy left the house. Dad was staying home with the toddler, mom would go to T.J.'s class and Rachel would go to Lucy's class and take notes. Sebastian was to return home as soon as his class was over to help out with Greg, so Dad could go back to campus and be there for Rachel's nine o'clock class. Sebastian didn't mind. Maybe

Greg would still be asleep and he could snag a nap himself, although still sleeping at nine o'clock would be a record for Greg.

♫

Mr. Bolkosky did not seem to suffer from Thursday morning sleepiness. He was all energy and optimism and humor. Even though it was not a piece written for a dance, Mr. Bolkosky had developed dance steps to go with May's Handel Sonata, and he made Bayly dance with him. Then he made Hunter and Sebastian dance with him too. During Hunter's *Gigue*, he showed them all some gigue steps and May, Bayly, Sebastian and Mr. Bolkosky danced them while Hunter played. The teacher invited the parents to join in, but nobody wanted to. Mr. Petersen pushed Blake to the front and May grabbed his hand and showed him what to do. She found it easier to dance when she was helping a little kid than when she was by herself.

Although it seemed like his focus was on fun and not the music, Mr. Bolkosky had the violinists thinking about tempo and dynamics, asking them to speed up, slow down, play more loudly or softly, seemingly based on the dance, but according to the written dynamics. Afterward, whenever May played that Handel Sonata, she would picture them dancing and remember the dynamics perfectly.

For *La Folia*, he had Bayly and Sebastian play together, keeping together. Whenever they played a run the dancers had to run in place, keeping time to the music.

They all agreed afterward that it was one of the most fun lessons they had ever had.

After A class, Sebastian hurried home and Hunter went with Blake to his lesson. Bayly and May decided to practice on the little hill outside the CCC. Bayly showed May the movements that go with the *Theme from "Witches' Dance,"* twirling at certain places, playing while squatting, playing on tiptoes, playing with the bow upside down, and then finishing with arms in the air and shouting, "Hey!" May loved the movements and they did it several times together, with other students joining them until they had a group of about twelve.

As they were packing to head to their C class, Mrs. Hall said, "Oh! I need to go back to the room. I forgot something."

"What did you forget?" asked Bayly.

"I'll just be a minute. Go on without me."

Bayly wrinkled up her face and said to May, "My mom is acting so strange today. She woke up all cheerful, and now she's missing one of my classes. She is usually totally uptight about going to all my classes and lessons and taking notes and stuff."

Mrs. Wong said, "It's OK. I said I'd take notes and share them with her."

In C class they worked on the pieces they would be playing for the Friday concert. The teacher focused on starting together, ending together, and keeping the same dynamics. As a group, they were pretty advanced students, so Bayly was surprised by how many of them kept losing focus and looking at places other than the teacher. They had to re-play the end of *Hu-*

moresque about twenty times until everyone finished at the same time.

Bayly saw her mom arrive in the class when there were only about ten minutes to go. She sat down and talked with Mrs. Wong for the rest of the class—something that was also very unusual. Mrs. Hall was normally silent during a class. Many times she had told Bayly that parents who talked during their children's classes were rude and distracting. And now she was doing it. Bayly watched closely and saw how energetic and animated her mom was. Mrs. Wong's face, at one point, looked both startled and joyful. What was going on?

Suddenly Bayly realized that she was still playing although everyone else had their bows in the air. Darn! The teacher made everyone start over again. Bayly returned her focus to the leader and hoped nobody noticed that she had messed up.

Bayly, May, Sebastian and Hunter had all left their violin cases in the same area where Bayly's mom and Mrs. Wong were sitting. As Bayly put her stuff away, she said to her mom, "I can't believe you were so late and then talked all through the end of the class. What's going on?"

Mrs. Hall merely smiled and waved away Bayly's criticisms. "I've invited your friends to join us for lunch."

May looked at her mom. Mrs. Wong nodded. "You and I will both go."

"Hunter," said Mrs. Hall, "your dad said that he and Blake had other plans but that you are free to join us. Why don't you talk to him before we leave?

And, Sebastian, I called your home and your dad said it was fine but he wanted you to tell your mom about it. She should be in the orchestra room with T.J."

"OK," said Sebastian. "I'll run over there right now. Will you watch my violin?"

Mrs. Hall nodded and Sebastian ran out the door. The orchestra room was on the same floor, just a couple of hallways away.

♫

They all walked to the Tokyo Steak House together. When they arrived, the hostess led them to a special reserved room. Waiting for them was Bayly's home violin teacher, Mrs. Bishop, as well as Mr. Harry and Janet.

Bayly looked at her mom. "What's going on?"

"Can't you guess?"

Bayly felt her heart hiccup. She walked hesitantly to the corner of the room where Mr. Harry stood smiling. There on the floor was an open violin case, with a Goldin violin inside. Suddenly her heart felt like it was riding a roller coaster. All the hairs on her arm were standing on end. Bayly bent over, picked up the violin, and held it close to her face to examine it. The warm sunshine color bronzed her face and tears ran down her cheeks. Grasping the violin firmly by the neck, Bayly did a jig with her feet, singing, "Yes! Yes! Yes!"

"Is that her Goldin?" asked May.

"Did you catch who stole it?" asked Hunter at the same time.

"As it turned out, nobody stole it," said Janet.

"It was partially my fault," said Mrs. Hall.

"Oh no!" interrupted Mr. Harry. "I am entirely responsible for this whole mix-up. I made a dreadful error at the airport."

Bayly stopped dancing and looked at her mom. "At the airport?"

Mrs. Hall nodded. "You remember those calls I kept getting and ignoring, saying I'd left a bag on the plane?"

"I was the one who left a bag on the plane," said Mr. Harry, waving his hand toward the violin case. "I brought four violins with me from California, two Goldins and two others. When we left the plane, we only had three. I thought Janet was carrying two and I was carrying two, but we left one behind."

Bayly stared at the violin in her hands. "But I played it in the store. It was there."

Janet shook her head. "That was my mistake. You played Peter Tolbert's violin. Because it was open when you came in, I didn't check the name tag on the case. After you left, I put away the chin rest and bow, and my dad closed the case and put the violin away behind the tables. He knew it was Peter's violin and Mr. Bolkosky had called to say he couldn't pick it up until a little later."

Mr. Harry said, "I had very carefully labeled each case with the customer's name and phone number. Unfortunately, I hadn't put any of my own information on the cases. I was merely transporting them from Augustina Goldin to her paying customer."

Mrs. Hall nodded. "That's why the airline kept calling me. There was only my name on the violin case."

Mrs. Wong said, "Wow! So that expensive violin was in lost luggage at the airport for four days?"

"Every time they called," explained Mrs. Hall, "I was in class and had my cell phone off. I never returned the messages because I hadn't been on a plane and I assumed it was some mistake. Then last night, at the talent show, my phone rang and a United agent finally got a hold of me. When she said it was a violin case, I started wondering. When she said, yes, it was a very yellow violin, I thought it must be the missing Goldin. I called Mr. Harry right away, and we arranged for the airline to bring the violin to his store this morning."

"Why didn't you tell me last night?" asked Bayly.

"I didn't want to get your hopes up," answered Mrs. Hall. "It seemed likely that it would be your Goldin, but what if it was some other mistake? Wasn't it a good surprise? And now, we can have a celebration party."

"Can I play it now?"

Mrs. Hall looked around the restaurant. "I think you should probably wait."

In a disappointed voice, Bayly said, "OK." Then smiling so big her eyes disappeared, she said, "I can't believe I finally have it!"

Everyone sat down. The Tokyo Steak House was one of those Japanese restaurants where the food is cooked right in front of the diners. Mrs. Hall ordered a lot of different kinds of meat and shrimp and vegetables to be cooked. The chef tossed the food around, juggling his knife and spatula, spinning salt and pepper shakers through the air. He squirted a sauce on some of the cooking meat with a bottle that looked like a little boy, peeing the sauce out. Hunter and Sebastian both laughed hysterically but May and Bayly said, "Eww!"

When they were walking back to campus, Hunter ran up and walked beside May. "One mystery solved and one mystery to go."

"Selena Montoya?" asked May.

"Yeah," said Hunter. "We really only have two more days to figure it out. By this time on Saturday we'll all be gone."

May shook her head. "I can't believe how fast this week is going."

Behind them, Bayly carried her Goldin violin and talked with Sebastian.

"Well, we didn't go swimming today. That only leaves tomorrow for the high dive."

Sebastian objected, "No it doesn't. Remember? I live here. I can do it anytime."

Bayly shook her head. "It doesn't count if I don't get to see it. Tomorrow, OK?"

"Maybe," answered Sebastian.

♫

After their afternoon classes, the four friends decided to attend the four o'clock recital in Michelsen Concert Hall. It was the last four o'clock concert of the week. When they walked in the door of the concert hall, they realized they were some of the first people to arrive. Hunter wanted them to spread out so each of them could try to sit by a teen that might say something about Selena Montoya, but Bayly refused.

"We don't have that much more time together. Let's sit together."

Sebastian and May agreed with Bayly, so there was nothing Hunter could do.

"Well, then let's not sit down right away. Maybe we can see Selena arrive and sit behind her."

All four of them stood awkwardly on the landing between the bottom level of seats and the upper level of seats. Just when Bayly was about to complain that they wouldn't be able to sit together if they waited any longer, Selena walked in. She and purple hair girl went down toward the stage. They sat in the second row, on the left side, behind the seats where the performers sit.

"Quick," said Hunter. He dashed down the aisle steps, pushing aside a mom and daughter.

"Hunter!" said May following him down. She stopped and apologized to the two that Hunter had bumped. Sebastian and Bayly followed close behind.

The four friends were able to sit directly behind the Selena Montoya girl.

"Did anyone grab a program?" asked Bayly.

They all looked at each other. Nobody had.

"I'll go get some," said Sebastian.

The teen girls in front of them were talking, but quietly so that it was impossible to hear what they were saying. Then, from a sloping entryway off to the side, spiky hair boy walked up to the seats where the performers sit and put his violin case on the floor. His hair had been gelled down so it wasn't spiky. He was wearing black slacks, a black button shirt and a black tie.

"Wow!" said May. "He looks really different. He must be performing."

When Sebastian came back with the programs, they looked to see who he might be.

"He must be the last performer," suggested May. "The violinist doing *Meditation* from 'Thais.' His name is Anthony Goldman and he's from Madison, Wisconsin."

"How do you know he's not this guy?" said Hunter, pointing to the second to last performer.

"Look underneath, that guy plays the cello. And he's not Margaret or Diane," May said, pointing at other names on the program. "And those two younger boys are probably playing the Bach Gavotte and *Minuet III*."

Hunter nodded and smiled at May. "You are quite the detective, aren't you?"

May giggled.

"Shh," said Bayly as the lights dimmed.

The performers had been chosen by their A teachers earlier in the week because of the strength of their playing. May thought it must be terrifying to play in front of such a large crowd. Her informal recital had had an audience of fifteen or twenty people, mostly the parents and friends of the performers. This concert hall was packed. There were maybe three or four hundred people in the audience.

After each performance, the audience applauded loudly. It was obvious where the performers' friends and families were sitting, as little clusters of people would whoop and shout more than others.

Spiky hair, or maybe they should call him gel hair boy went last. His violin was a Goldin, but now they knew it wasn't Bayly's Goldin. The sound seemed to flow into the warm gold color and melt the air around May. She had always loved *Meditation* from "Thais," but she had never heard it like this before: the Goldin, the appreciative crowd, her friends around her. Heaven must feel like this, she thought. When Anthony Goldman was finished, May jumped up and whooped, surprising Hunter.

In front of them, the two teen girls also jumped up, and screamed as well. The Selena girl raised her arms and swayed and her name tag flew over her shoulder. It was right in front of May's eyes: Stacy Moore.

"Look!" May grabbed Hunter's arm and yanked him up, but the girl had already pulled on her name tag string, returning it to her front.

"What?" asked Hunter.

"Nothing," said May, thinking. "I'll tell you later." But would she? Would he be too disappointed? It was so fun the way they played detective together. Did she want to spoil that?

♫

Bayly turned the tuning pegs again. Her E string kept going off. When it was in tune, she put the violin to her shoulder and started playing again. Mrs. Hall looked up from her magazine. "You've been playing for more than an hour Bayly, don't you want to do something else tonight? There's the teen orchestra concert at seven o'clock. I'm pretty sure Hunter and May are planning to go to it."

Bayly put the violin down on its case and breathed a deep sigh of happiness. "I guess I should do something else. I just love this violin so much. Thank you Mom!" Filled with emotion, Bayly lunged toward her mother's bed and hugged her mom, crushing her magazine and knocking off her reading glasses.

Mrs. Hall laughed and then stood. Finding her glasses on the bed she folded them and put them away.

At the concert, they found seats by Hunter and May who were pouring over the program.

"I don't see her name listed," said Hunter.

"Are you looking for Selena Montoya?" asked Bayly.

Hunter nodded. "I saw her getting ready with the rest of the teens, so I know she's here."

Bayly looked at May who seemed nervous and kept looking away.

"I never thought she was Selena Montoya," said Bayly. "What would Selena Montoya be doing in Stevens Point, Wisconsin?"

"Playing the violin?" giggled May.

Bayly laughed too.

Hunter responded, "Have either of you ever even watched *A Girl in the City*?"

May said, "I think I saw it once."

Bayly shook her head.

"So as far as I'm concerned your opinions don't really matter," said Hunter.

The orchestra members filed onto the stage and the program began.

After the concert, the kids decided to meet in the Hansen Hall basement where people sometimes played games in the evening.

"I need to stop by my room first," said Bayly. "I'll meet you there."

A little while later, Bayly and Mrs. Hall walked down to the basement which was a sort of open lounge area. They saw a group of kids sitting on the floor playing spoons, but May and Hunter weren't among them. Instead, Bayly saw her friends sitting at a table, playing a card game with a few other kids. Mrs. Wong and another parent were also playing. Bayly pulled up a chair and squeezed between May and a boy named Dirk; Mrs. Hall sat by Mrs. Wong.

"What are you playing?" Bayly asked May.

"WhooNu. Ever played it?"

"No."

"Well, what happens is everyone gets four cards, like these." May showed Bayly some cards. One said Jigsaw Puzzles, one said Chocolate Cake, and one said Hollywood. "One person doesn't get any cards. That person is the Whosit. You look at your cards and you guess which thing the Whosit would like best. You put it in the card holder. Then everyone else does the same thing. When everyone has turned in a card, the Whosit looks at all the cards and ranks them from best to worst. See, John is doing it now. The goal is to have your card be the best, or at least high up."

John had lined up his cards so that you couldn't see what the words were. He said, "I don't know who put this one in, but I definitely do not like unicorns." Everyone laughed as he turned over a card that said Unicorns. He turned over the cards one by one until he got to his favorite: snowboarding.

John cleared off the cards from the middle of the table and everyone passed their cards. "Give cards to Bayly and her mom," said May.

"Who's the Whosit?" Mrs. Wong asked.

"I am," said Hunter.

Bayly looked at her cards. UFOs, Jazz, Oysters, Stuffed Animals. She looked at Hunter for a few minutes. Would he like jazz? What about oysters? He didn't seem like the kind of kid who would try weird food. What about UFOs? Who exactly liked UFOs? She sighed. It didn't seem like her choices were very good. She picked Jazz and slid it into the pile of cards people were offering.

Hunter picked up the pile and browsed through his choices. He laughed and said, "No way. Hmmm. This is hard. I think I know who gave me this one." He looked at May. Finally he arranged his cards on the table.

Jazz came out in the middle. May won with Mysteries. "I got lucky," she said. "I had the perfect card."

They played several more rounds until their parents forced them to quit and go to bed.

Friday

"Hurry, we're going to be late," said Sebastian, trying to get his dad out of T.J's classroom.

"Everything set?" Mr. Phelps checked with T.J. "I'll be back before your class is over. OK, go on up now."

Mr. Phelps moved to the door and followed Sebastian out into the NFAC hall and toward the stairwell. "This is unusual," Mr. Phelps said, laughing. "A child trying to hurry a parent. I think we have things backward here."

Sebastian was not amused. "You missed every A class this week. I don't want to be late for the only one you're going to."

"I'm hurrying; I'm hurrying," said his dad, realizing how serious Sebastian was taking the morning. Today would be the hardest for the Phelps family, who owned only one camera but wanted to take pictures of each of their children with each of their children's teachers. There would be a lot of running around and not much attention to the actual classes. Really, they should have remembered this from last year and started taking pictures earlier in the week. Fortunately, Sebastian and Rachel were in the same orchestra, which helped a little. Also, there was a break from classes in the middle of the day and the family could relax, eat lunch and swim. The wagon that had been left at T.J.'s classroom contained sack lunches and swimsuits for everyone.

"You know," said Sebastian, opening the door to the CCC. "We wouldn't have this problem if we had a cell phone with a camera."

Mr. Phelps said, "No, then we'd just have a whole lot of extra problems, like paying cell phone bills, and people calling me when I'd rather not be called. I hate talking on the phone at home. Why would I want a phone I would carry around with me?"

"Well, I like talking on the phone. You don't have to have a cell phone; you could just get one for me."

"When you go off to college, I'm sure we'll do that," answered Mr. Phelps.

Sebastian rolled his eyes. This was the answer he always got when he begged his parents for a cell phone.

They entered the room quietly and found seats against the wall. May had already started playing her Sonata. Sebastian looked around the room. Bayly and Hunter were sitting next to each other in chairs closer to the front of the room. In the chair next to Bayly sat a large garden gnome looking as if he were watching May play. Sebastian squinted his eyes and tried to figure out what it was doing there, then he had to hold back a snort. The gnome was so ridiculous looking.

When May finished, Sebastian stood up.

"Can I go next?" he asked Mr. Bolkosky. "My dad can't stay the whole time, but he wanted to watch today's lesson and take a picture of us together."

Mr. Bolkosky looked at Hunter and Bayly and the gnome. "Is that all right with you guys?" Hunter and Bayly nodded. The gnome just stared straight ahead.

Sebastian giggled. "What's with the gnome?"

Mr. Bolkosky's face held a serious expression. "He's my only friend and often comes with me to institute, but he is shy and has trouble coming out until the last day. He does like to have his picture taken, though, so if you would like, he could join us in the picture your dad takes."

Sebastian grinned. "Sure."

May and Bayly giggled. Bayly said, "I want pictures with him too."

Still serious, Mr. Bolkosky said, "I think he would agree to that."

Sebastian played all of *La Folia* today, focusing on the runs, the dynamics and all the things they had been working on all week. When he finished, everyone applauded.

Mr. Phelps moved forward. "I hate to interrupt the flow of the class, but could we do the picture right now so that I can run back to the NFAC and get pictures of my other children and their teachers?"

"Certainly. How should we pose, Sebastian? I rather like the sideways, looking off in the distance like we are thinking serious, great thoughts." Mr. Bolkosky struck that pose.

"Perfect."

"And with my friend?" asked Mr. Bolkosky.

"Of course," said Sebastian.

Mr. Bolkosky picked up the gnome and placed him on the desk at the front of the room, angling the gnome's body so he was looking off to the side. Sebastian and Mr. Bolkosky stood next to him, serious faces, also looking off to the side. Mr. Phelps took a photo while everyone else laughed.

"And now, one as friends," said Mr. Bolkosky.

He turned the gnome to face Mr. Phelps. Sebastian stood on one side of the plaster man and Mr. Bolkosky on the other. They put their arms on each other's shoulders, wrapping the gnome in a half-hug.

"Smile," said Mr. Phelps. Sebastian and Mr. Bolkosky smiled. The gnome kept the same expression.

Mr. Phelps held out his hand to Mr. Bolkosky. "Thank you so much."

"I'm glad I got a chance to meet you," said Mr. Bolkosky, shaking his hand. "You have a wonderful son and violinist. I enjoyed working with him this week."

"Well, I know he really enjoyed your class. He talked about it all the time. Sorry I have to run." Mr. Phelps turned toward Sebastian, "See you after in T.J.'s room, right?"

Hunter went next, and Bayly was last. She had brought her Goldin.

"Well, well," said Mr. Bolkosky. "Can I see it?"

Bayly handed the golden instrument to him. He strummed the strings with his thumb and put his ear to the F hole. With each strum he took a slow, careful step toward the door. Suddenly, he stopped strumming and moving and looked at Bayly.

"Afraid I'm going to walk off with it?" he joked.

Bayly walked over to where he stood by the door and took the Goldin from his hands. "A little."

"Smart girl," said Mr. Bolkosky. "You shouldn't trust anyone with this beauty. I take it you're going to play it today?"

"You bet!" said Bayly.

She began her piece, the minor notes slow and sad. This was Sebastian's piece, too, so he was intimately familiar with the slow sad beginning, and yet the notes coming from the Goldin were a new kind of sadness. So deep, so full and lonely, it made his heart ache. As Bayly played, her audience held its breath, the sound of her bow on string the only thing moving in the room. Twice she had to stop and re-tune a string, giving everyone a chance to exhale and then, when she started again, the magic began all over. When she finished, Bayly bowed deeply, her long hair falling down into her face. Hunter, May and Sebastian stood up to applaud and Hunter whooped.

Mr. Bolkosky crossed to where Bayly stood and gave her a hug. "I know you want to credit your new violin for this spectacular performance, but your hard work this week is the real reason for your improvement."

Then it was picture time and everyone took turns posing with the gnome, with Mr. Bolkosky, with each other. Mrs. Hall took a picture of Bayly kissing the gnome, with Mr. Bolkosky frowning in the background. Bayly pulled Sebastian into the group and the parents took pictures of all the kids together.

"We can email you the pictures," said Mr. Petersen.

Sebastian nodded. "Thanks. And my parents can take pictures of all of us together after the concert tonight. I better go now." He rushed out the CCC to the NFAC where his family needed him to watch Greg.

Bayly turned to Hunter and May. "You guys are going swimming today, right? I think I've just about talked Sebastian into going off the high dive."

"Sure," said May.

"I don't know. I might be doing something else," said Hunter.

Bayly wrinkled her eyes and then turned to May. "Talk him into it, OK? We should all be there to make sure Sebastian does it." Bayly left with her mom.

May picked up her violin case and started walking out the door with Hunter.

"What do you mean you might be doing something else?" asked May. "I thought swimming was one of your favorite things about institute."

"Well, yeah, but—"

Mr. Petersen turned around from far down the hallway. "Hunter, hurry. It's almost time for Blake's class."

"I gotta go," said Hunter. "I'll tell you about it at C class."

♫

May got to C class early, tuned up and got on stage. Hunter arrived a few minutes later. He got on stage without tuning up. May noticed but chose not to say anything.

"So, why don't you want to go swimming?"

"I've got this plan about Selena," said Hunter smiling. "Today's my last day to find out if she is really Selena Montoya or not. I'm going to get to DeBot cafeteria when it first opens and stay all through lunch. She's bound to eat sometime. When I see her, I'm just going to go right up to her and ask."

May frowned. She had hoped she wouldn't have to tell Hunter, or that he would figure it out for himself. But, she didn't want him to waste the whole middle of his day.

"She isn't Selena Montoya," said May.

"Well, probably not," said Hunter, "but I've got to find out for sure."

"No," said May. "I mean, I know for sure. At the concert last night, when spiky hair boy finished playing, her name tag flew over her shoulder and I saw her name. It's Stacy Moore."

Hunter cocked his head in disbelief. "Are you making that up so I'll go swimming? Why didn't you tell me yesterday?"

May hung her head. "I don't know. After I saw her name, I felt so bad for you. And, we'd had so much fun spying on her. I just couldn't tell you."

A shadow crossed Hunter's eyes.

May tried to look at him, hoping he wasn't mad at her, but just then the teacher called for everyone's attention. May was made to move to the front of the group of students so she could see. All through the class she worried that Hunter was mad at her. After class, things were a little crazy as everyone tried to get pictures with the teacher. Hunter was gone before she had a chance to talk to him.

Bayly touched May on the shoulder. "Are you coming swimming now?"

May turned to where her mom was talking to Mrs. Hall. "Can I go swimming now?" asked May.

Mrs. Wong nodded. "I'm going to that eleven o'clock lecture I told you about, but I'll meet you at the pool so we can go to eat together."

Mrs. Hall said, "I was planning to go to a lecture as well, but something else has come up so I can't."

Mrs. Wong nodded. "I'll see you at lunch, May."

"OK," said May.

Mrs. Hall, Bayly and May left the NFAC and headed across campus, toward the dorms and the swimming pool building.

"I've got to go back to the dorm to change into my suit," said Bayly. "Do you have yours with you?"

May shook her head. "No, I've got to go back too."

Mrs. Hall said, "I've got my book and I'm not going to swim, so I'll see you at the pool."

Bayly and Mrs. Hall's eyes met like they had some sort of secret, then Mrs. Hall turned and went another direction. The two girls walked on toward the dorms.

"OK," said Bayly. "Let's hurry, May. Hunter and Sebastian are going to meet us at the pool."

May's eyes lit up. "Did you talk to Hunter? He's going swimming?"

"Of course," said Bayly. "Hunter loves to swim. It's Sebastian I had to talk into meeting us there. He's still nervous about the high dive."

"Do you think he'll do it?" asked May.

Bayly nodded with confidence. "I made a deal with him, so I'm sure he'll do it."

"What deal?"

Bayly shook her head. "I can't tell, but you'll find out when he does the high dive."

The girls hurried across campus to get their suits.

♫

Sebastian stood at the foot of the ladder to the high dive. This is crazy, he thought. Even if I do this and survive, my parents will probably say no. Then it will have been for nothing.

Sebastian looked over to the bleachers where Mrs. Hall sat next to his mom. Without his glasses, they were a little fuzzy, but he could tell they were talking. Were they talking about it right now? Mrs. Phelps smiled and waved at him. Would she be smiling if they were talking about it? Probably not.

"Hey, you gonna go, or not?" asked a kid.

"Oh, sorry," said Sebastian, moving away from the ladder. He really shouldn't be standing there anyway. If he jumped before the others got here, nobody would believe him.

Hunter came out of the locker room with his dad and brother. They all wore swimsuits. The whole Petersen family came toward Sebastian and the diving boards.

"Hi, Sebastian," said Mr. Petersen. "We were just talking about having a cannonball contest. Want to join in?"

"Sure," said Sebastian.

They got in line for the short diving board closest to the bleachers.

Hunter, who had been talking to Mrs. Phelps and Mrs. Hall, joined the boys in the diving board line. Hunter said, "The moms said they'll judge but if anyone gets them wet that person automatically loses."

"Ha!" said Mr. Petersen. "That's a challenge I can't pass up."

Blake went first and his splash was pretty good, considering he was so small. Mr. Petersen's splash was enormous, and though water did come out of the pool onto the tiled floor, none of it reached the bleachers.

"Ah," the dad said, "I'll have to do better next time."

They took several turns until the girls arrived. May walked over and started talking to Hunter right away. Sebastian didn't pay them any attention. Instead, he watched as Bayly walked up to the bleachers and talked to her mom and his mom. Then Sebastian's mom got up and walked across the pool area to the shallow end where his dad was playing with T.J. and Lucy. They talked for a few minutes and Mrs. Phelps returned to the bleachers.

Bayly walked over to where Sebastian, May and the Petersens stood.

"It's all set," said Bayly. "You ready to go off the high dive?"

"Are you serious?" asked Sebastian. "There's no way my parents agreed to it."

"They did," grinned Bayly. "My mom explained everything to them, and they are totally OK with it."

Sebastian's stomach flipped. He'd wanted it for so long, and he was going to have to jump off the high dive to get it. He took a deep breath.

"I can do it."

We walked toward the ladder for the high dive.

"Do you know what the deal is?" May asked Hunter.

"What deal?" asked Hunter.

"Never mind," said May.

They all stood and watched Sebastian climb up the steps.

Halfway up, Sebastian paused. He'd made it to the top once before but had turned back and climbed down instead of jumping. Today he wasn't going to do that. He took another deep breath and climbed to the top.

Sebastian held tightly to the cold metal handrail at the top. The board was really the same board as the one he had just been on. Greenish white plastic stuff, sandpaper-like surface. He could pretend it was just like the other board. He looked off to the side. The pool was a lot farther down. Slowly, he walked to the middle of the board. Here, he could still hold on to the handrails. One more step and he wouldn't have the rail anymore. The thought made him dizzy. He needed to go fast. Once he let go of the handrail, he had to take the two or three steps to the edge and jump right away. He wanted to be in charge of his jump. He didn't want to fall because he was dizzy. His heart was beating so fast, he felt it pounding in his ears.

Sebastian took another, very deep breath. Then he moved. In two quick, deliberate steps he was at the end of the board and in the same movement he was over the edge. He held his nose closed with one hand and kept the other arm close to the side of his body. He tried to keep his body as straight as a knife. Before it seemed possible, he was in the water and going deep, deep into the pool. His ears popped. Quick as a dolphin, he kicked his legs and swam to the surface. He breathed in the humid air and heard applause. His friends and family were all standing at the side of the pool clapping. Sebastian felt his face flush.

He'd done it! It hadn't been bad at all. In fact, it was fun. He wanted to do it again.

Sebastian swam to the edge and climbed out. "Who wants to go with me, this time?"

Bayly and May laughed.

"Listen to him!" said Mrs. Phelps.

"You can go as many more times as you want," said Mr. Phelps, "but you only get one cell phone."

May turned to Bayly, "He got a cell phone for jumping?"

Bayly giggled and nodded. "My uncle works for URfone and gave me some free minute cards. He thinks we use URfones, but my mom and dad are on a different plan, so we don't need the cards. Sebastian still has to buy the phone, but URfones are cheap."

"Man, I'm so jealous," said May.

"I can give you some cards too. Just talk your mom into buying you a phone. If we all have phones, then we can stay in touch texting each other. Texting is cheaper than calling."

May shook her head. "I don't know. I've been working really hard to get her to let me have an email account, but she won't let me have that."

Bayly looked surprised. "You don't have email either? My mom should talk to your mom. I know some parents are paranoid about having their kids on the internet, but cell phones are different. I mean, what if there's an emergency? Your mom should want you to have a cell phone. And only the people who have your number can call you. How can that be dangerous? Besides, you have to pay when somebody calls you, so you'll be careful not to give your number to very many people."

May was nodding enthusiastically. "Please, have your mom talk to my mom."

Suddenly there was a loud smacking noise and a large wave crested out of the pool, soaking Bayly and May where they stood talking. Shrieks and laughter erupted from the bleachers. The moms sitting there had also been splashed. May turned back to the pool to see Mr. Petersen swimming toward the side. When he got there, he asked, "Did I get them?"

Hunter laughed. "You got 'em wet, Dad. Did you see that?" Hunter asked May and Bayly. "My dad just did a cannonball off the high dive."

May's mouth fell open.

"Did it hurt?" asked Bayly.

"Nah," said Mr. Petersen, but when he climbed out of the pool both girls noticed how red his back was.

"Your dad is crazy," said Bayly.

"But not as crazy as me," said Hunter, jumping high in the air, grabbing one knee and sticking out his tongue. When he landed in the water, the splash he made soaked the girls once again.

Bayly jumped in right away and dunked him when his head came up. May looked around for Sebastian and was just in time to see him jump off the high dive. She smiled and dove into the deep water.

♫

May had lunch with Hunter, eating fast between swimming and their orchestra concert. They didn't see the Selena Montoya girl, and neither of them mentioned her.

Over the past week, their orchestra had met daily and some parents had stayed to listen, but many parents had done different things during that time. Now, on the last day, the students would put on a concert for the parents. For the first part of Friday's class, Mr. Poffinbarger had them work on the parts of each piece that had been the shakiest.

Now, the room was filled with siblings and parents, many holding video cameras. For the first time, May felt exposed in her orchestra piece. She and Bayly were in the middle of the first violin section, but Bayly's Goldin changed everything. The harsh fluorescent lighting lit the room in a white/purple glare, but Bayly's yellow violin seemed to emit a warm, buttery glow. May felt bathed in its light and imagined everyone was looking at them. Her stomach crawled with nerves until she realized that if everyone was looking at Bayly's Goldin, then they were really looking at

Bayly and not May. Her stomach calmed just as Mr. P. lifted his baton.

♫

After the concert, May wanted to get her friends in the picture she took with Mr. P. That way it would be more like an orchestra photo. She tugged on them all to get in the photo and included Sebastian's sister Rachel who had played with the second violins.

As they walked out of the orchestra room, Mrs. Wong put her arm around her daughter. "One more class and then just the final concert. Has it been a good week, Honey?"

May hugged her mom, "It's been great. I'm going to be so sad when it's over."

♫

In B class, they worked on the pieces they would be playing in the concert that evening. Each student had received in A class a sticker with a number on it to wear on his or her shirt. The students would gather in different rooms in the CCC, based on which pieces they knew, and then walk in a specific order across the street to Quandt Gym, where the concert would be held. Sebastian, Hunter, Bayly and May all had the same number for their shirts and would meet in the same room.

"I'm glad we'll get to be next to each other," May told Hunter.

Before photo-taking time, the teacher handed out special cards for each of the twelve students. They had her name and email and a quote from Dr. Suzuki, "Knowledge is not skill. Knowledge plus ten thousand times is skill."

♫

Before dinner, Mrs. Wong made May pack up most of her things. They had to leave early in the morning to catch their eight o'clock flight. After getting things organized, they went to the cafeteria for dinner. As she ate, May felt melancholy. She watched all the people she knew come and go at the cafeteria. Hunter and his family arrived just as Mrs. Wong and May were putting their trays away.

"Can I sit and talk with Hunter, even though I'm done?" May asked her mom.

"Sure. Mrs. Hall asked me to stop by her room after dinner, so I might go over there for a little while. Wait for me at the room, though. I'll be back before we need to leave for the concert."

May was glad her mom was going to talk to Mrs. Hall, but she had little hope that her mom would agree to a cell phone. May walked over to the dessert area and grabbed an ice cream. Still feeling blue, May sat next to Blake and across from Hunter.

Hunter was as lively and goofy as ever, and before she knew it, May was laughing and enjoying herself.

♫

They walked into Quandt gym in single file. The bleachers were full of parents and others to watch the final violin concert.

In the CCC room their teacher had told them to meet in, there had been about fifteen kids. A teacher had organized them into a single file line and Bayly had made sure the four of them stuck together. Now they were all in the line with Bayly, Sebastian, Hunter and May following and being followed by lots of violinists. In fact, there were probably two or three hundred violinists in all.

The gym floor had been covered with a rubbery brown tarp and masking tape had been attached to make a grid. The kids at the front of the line walked all the way to the front of the grid and children began sitting down where masking tape lines intersected.

Unfortunately, Bayly and Sebastian got the last two spots on one row and Hunter and May had to walk down the row behind them, ending up in a different area.

Before May sat down, she waved at Bayly, who shrugged as if to say, "I tried to keep us together."

May looked down at the place on the floor where she was supposed to sit and wished she'd worn a different dress. She dropped to her knees carefully and then slowly lowered herself to the ground, sitting with her legs bent and together just to her side. It wasn't easy to sit on the floor modestly while wearing a short dress. It was her favorite dress, and she had brought it especially for this concert. Who would have thought she'd be sitting on the floor in it? May realized now why Bayly had worn slacks, even though it was the final concert and everyone was supposed to be dressed up. She sighed. Next year she would know. Looking around, she saw that lots of girls were having the same problem she was having. Maybe it was a sacrifice some girls made to look nice.

"Hunter, how long will we be sitting on the floor?"

Hunter shrugged. "I don't know. Not long. We're pretty close to the front, so our pieces will start pretty soon."

To begin the concert, teens in the chamber music C class stood on the stage facing the kids on the floor and played several pieces.

Next, a small group of pre-twinkles and their parents came out on the stage. They were so small and so cute! Each parent put a foot chart on the stage and the child carefully placed his or her feet on the chart. Then the children did the "Up Like a Rocket, Down Like the Rain" bow exercise. One little boy was so enthusiastic, his bow was flying all over the place.

May couldn't help but laugh.

After the pre-twinkles the main part of the concert started. The first piece performed was a very advanced piece and May stayed sitting on the floor. The teens all stood on the stage and about four or five kids in the front row on the floor stood and played. The next piece was the first movement of the Bach Concerto in A minor. A large block of kids on the floor to the right of Hunter and May stood to play. The next piece was *Country Dance.* May and the block of kids around her stood and played. The concert progressed with easier pieces and more children standing until they got to the last piece: *Twinkle, Twinkle Little Star* and every violinist in the room was standing.

The audience applauded, and the concert was over.

"It's tape time," said Hunter.

"What?" asked May, but she figured it out before Hunter could say anything else. Children were ripping the masking tape from the floor and creating large tape balls. The younger children were much more aggressive, trying to get as much tape and as large a ball as possible. Tape balls were flying everywhere.

"Let's quick find our parents and put our violins away," said Hunter. "There's something I want to do."

They hurried through the kids on the floor toward where their parents were sitting in the bleachers. The moment her violin was safe in its case, Hunter grabbed her hand and dragged her away.

"I hope I'm not too late," he said.

"What are we doing?" May asked.

Hunter showed May the camera he was holding in his other hand, as if that were an explanation.

"There she is!" he cried, pulling May around a group of parents talking to one of the teachers. Suddenly May found herself standing in front of the Selena Montoya girl.

"Can we take a picture with you?" Hunter was saying.

May felt her face get hot. Why was he asking her this?

"Sure," the girl said, smiling. "Hey, Tony, come take a picture of us."

Spiky hair boy took the camera from Hunter's hand and backed off.

The Selena girl put her arms around Hunter and May and pulled them close.

"Say cheese curds," said Spiky Hair boy.

May started laughing but Hunter and the Selena girl both said, "Cheese curds."

"Thanks a lot," said Hunter, taking his camera back.

"Yeah, thanks," said May, then to Hunter she said, "We should get pictures with Bayly and Sebastian while we're all dressed up."

People roamed the gym floor, saying final goodbyes, taking pictures, and throwing masking tape balls.

"I can't believe it's over," May said to her mother.

"I heard some parents talking about ordering pizza and playing games in the basement lounge tonight. We should go back and join in."

May talked Bayly into meeting them at their dorm, and Sebastian was allowed to join them too.

"May!" someone called. May looked around and saw Hunter beckoning her over from the bleachers. "Come on, I want to show you something."

May looked around. Almost everybody was gone. "Well, I guess," she said. Hunter pulled her under the bleachers.

"Look at this," Hunter whispered.

"Look at wha—wow!" May saw some folded money stuck in between two bars over their heads. "Cool, but how do we get it?"

"Um." Hunter looked around the gym. "There," he said and ran over to a corner where he picked up a tape ball. "Like this."

Breathing fast he walked over toward the money. Then, with surprising accuracy, he threw the tape ball into the air where it stuck on the bottom of the bleacher right above the money. With a groan of frustration Hunter kicked a bar under the bleachers which caused the tape ball to swing back and forth and then drop onto the bills. The money stuck to the tape ball and then fell from the bleachers. May caught the bundle.

"Wow! This is amazing. Here, you take it," she said holding out the money to Hunter.

Unfolding it, Hunter straightened two one-dollar bills. He handed one to May, saying, "We should share. And, I've got one more thing to give you."

He reached into his pocket and pulled out a pink butterfly bow creature. "I saw your mom didn't buy it for you at the institute store, so I got it for you."

"Thank you!" May said giving Hunter a big hug.

"What's going on back here?" said a voice.

May and Hunter stepped away from each other. Sebastian and Bayly appeared beside the bleachers.

"We were ready to go back to your dorm to play games, but we couldn't find you," said Bayly looking at May and raising her eyebrows.

May held out the bow buddy. "Hunter gave this to me."

"Let's go," said Hunter, moving quickly away from the bleachers and toward the doors.

♫

Back at Hansen Hall they ate pizza and played spoons, Whoo-nu and Twister. Sebastian was the first to leave, saying he had to be home by eleven. Others trickled out and by midnight only Hunter, May, Bayly, Mrs. Hall and Mrs. Wong were left.

"We've got an early flight in the morning," said Mrs. Wong.

May yawned. "Yeah, I guess I better get to bed."

Hunter handed May a piece of paper. "It's my email and cell number," he said. "We should stay in touch."

"Yeah," said Bayly grabbing a pencil from a table. "Let me write mine down too." She wrote down her information and copied theirs onto another piece of paper. "I'll pass this on to Sebastian too."

Mrs. Hall said, "You should write down your postal addresses. Maybe you could actually write paper letters to each other."

Bayly glared at her mom, and May laughed, but they wrote down their postal addresses too.

Handing the paper to May, Bayly said, "This was the best institute ever. And not because I got my Goldin. I'm glad I got to be in an A class with you guys."

They hugged and Bayly left.

Hunter, May and Mrs. Wong walked upstairs together. Blake and Mr. Petersen had gone to bed earlier.

Outside their doors May said, "We probably won't see you in the morning. We have to leave early to catch our flight." She hugged Hunter. "Thanks for the bow buddy."

Hunter grinned. “Thanks for being my partner in detection. See you next year.”

May nodded and shut the door.

Saturday

May sat on one of the seats in the waiting area of the Central Wisconsin Airport. It was the smallest airport she'd ever been in, and she'd never been in such an empty airport. Their flight didn't leave for another hour, but May would have thought more people would be here.

"I'm going to see if there is a bookstore or anywhere to buy a magazine or something," said Mrs. Wong.

May looked up and around. She could see the entire waiting room and boarding area; there was obviously nothing like that.

"Are you going back through security, Mama?" asked May. "There's nothing here."

"Yes, but there aren't really any lines. Do you want to come with me?"

May shook her head. "I'll just wait here."

May was engrossed in her book when she noticed someone sit down right next to her. She looked up, expecting her mother, only to discover the Selena Montoya girl.

"Hi," the girl said.

May put her finger in her book to mark the spot and closed it. "Hi."

"I wanted to thank you and your boyfriend for being so cool last night," said the girl.

"Um, you're welcome," answered May, although she didn't know why the girl was thanking her.

"I was worried at first, but then you just walked away."

May wrinkled her forehead in confusion.

"I could tell you knew who I was when you helped me out with the water gun fight, but you didn't bother me or make a big deal out of it. Even when you asked for the picture, you were totally cool."

May was still confused. "But your name tag said something else. So you really are Selena Montoya?"

"Live and in person," she said, flashing her famous smile. "Selena Montoya is my stage name. My real name is Stacy Moore. It's been great hanging out in Wisconsin at institute. I wasn't sure how it would go. When I was here last year I wasn't famous. The institute friends I keep in touch with knew what happened, but they are all cool about it, and nobody else even recognized me, except you two." She took a deep breath, "I gotta sort of get myself back into the mode of being famous and recognized."

"You've come before to institute?" asked May.

"I've come to institute ever since I was a little kid."

May laughed nervously. "You know, I didn't think you were Selena Montoya. It was Hunter who was so sure you were. He's going to die when I tell him. Wait. He's been to institute a lot of times too. How come he didn't already know you?"

Stacy shrugged. "He's younger than me, so we were probably never in the same class. Plus, I used to wear glasses and have short hair. We probably had seen each other before and just not noticed."

"That makes sense," said May.

"I've got an idea," said Stacy reaching into her pocket. "Let's take another picture and send it to him." She took out her cell phone and held it in front of them. They put their heads together so their ears were touching.

"Pucker up," said Stacy.

"What?" said May, pulling her head out of the picture.

"Oh, come on, it'll be fun."

May got back in the picture and the two girls puckered their lips like they were going to kiss the camera. Stacy pressed the button.

"What's his number?"

"Oh, I've got it here," said May digging through her carry-on. She pulled out the paper with Hunter's cell phone number.

Stacy sent the photo with a text: Kisses from your girlfriends, May and Selena.

May covered her face with her hands saying, "I can't believe we did that." But she was giggling.

"Why not?" asked Selena, putting her phone away.

"He isn't really my boyfriend."

Selena smiled. "It'll give him something to think about until he sees you next year. You are coming back next year, aren't you?"

May nodded vigorously. "I wouldn't miss it!"

Authors' Notes

The Suzuki method of music education was developed by Dr. Shinichi Suzuki in the mid-twentieth century. Suzuki believed that all children have talent and will blossom when allowed to learn at their own pace, in a nurturing environment. He based this philosophy on the way babies learn their mother tongue. The learning of a language occurs naturally, with parents talking to their children, encouraging attempts at speech, and repeating words. Not all children start speaking at the same exact time, but every child does master a mother tongue. Learning to read occurs at a later stage, when the child is already proficient in his native language.

This educational philosophy is easily applied to learning a musical instrument. Suzuki students, starting as early as age three, listen repetitively to CDs of the music they are currently learning and will soon be learning. The Suzuki repertoire begins with simple pieces, the students learning specific skills, step by step, moving through the repertoire at the appropriate pace for the individual student. Reading music occurs after a certain level of proficiency in the student's musical instrument has occurred.

An important aspect of the Suzuki method of musical education is the learning triangle. The Suzuki method requires the active participation of the students' parents. Teachers, parents and students form the learning triangle. Parents attend the lessons of their students and learn from the teacher. At home, the parents are the teacher and guide the students in achieving the goals set by the teacher. As students mature, they learn to manage their practice time and become independent learners.

Margery Aber studied under Dr. Suzuki in 1967 and began using the Suzuki method in her teaching of the violin later that year at the University of Wisconsin–Stevens Point, starting one of the first Suzuki programs in America. In 1971, Miss Aber founded the American Suzuki Institute, modeled after Dr. Suzuki's summer school in Japan for teachers, parents and students. It provided a meeting place for the followers of the fledgling Suzuki movement in the U.S. The American Suzuki Institute takes place every year in August, hosting teachers and students of all levels, from around the world. It is the largest program of its kind outside of Japan. For more information, visit the American Suzuki Institute website at `http://www.uwsp.edu/cofac/suzuki/asi`.

Acknowledgments

The story told herein is fictitious, but the setting and some of the characters are real. We are grateful to Gabriel Bolkosky, Pat D'Ercole, Terry Durbin and David Poffinbarger for allowing us to portray them as fictional characters. Thanks also to Pat for encouragement and editing help, and to Jillian Noble for designing the cover.

About the Authors

Tom Felt has been a Suzuki violinist since 2004 and has been attending American Suzuki Institute for most of that time. He is also an avid reader.

Craig Felt has been a Suzuki violinist from the age of three and has spent many summers at ASI.

Andy Felt is a math professor at the University of Wisconsin–Stevens Point and is the Suzuki parent teacher in the Felt family.

Elizabeth Caulfield Felt teaches English composition at the University of Wisconsin–Stevens Point and has written two other novels, both for adults.

Also by Andy Felt

Math Vitamins for Suzuki Students
Inject Fun (and Math Skills) Into Your Practice
by Andy Felt and George Kung

This book contains directions for over fifty games to be played between a parent and child (age 3–7), providing a fun way to develop math skills and sense. Your kids will love to beat mom or dad at games, and won't even realize they are doing math. The games are ordered to bring the next skill along at just the right time. Directions for each game are short and easy to understand. A game board is provided.

See the The Suzuki Association of the Americas website to order:

`www.suzukiassociation.org/store`